HOW TO TAKE A TEST

by John E. Dobbin

CONTENTS

John E. Dobbin
1914–1979

It is with gratitude and pride that we dedicate *How to Take a Test* to its author, John E. Dobbin. Throughout his 29 years at Educational Testing Service, John's writing talent, imagination, and enthusiasm strengthened and enriched projects too numerous to mention here. His special interest, however, was in developing and writing a series of nontechnical books that would attempt to unravel the mystery of tests and testing for students, parents, school board members, and classroom teachers.

This book is the only one of the proposed series he was able to finish before his death in 1979. In *How to Take a Test*, we have a fine example of the author's robust style and his wise and witty way of deflating pomposity and pretension. Reading it, we once again admire the effort he put into all that he set out to do, we delight in his humanity and boundless good humor, and we cherish the memory of his friendship.

Thelma L. Spencer
Project Director
Educational Testing Service

PREFACE

As its title so boldly proclaims, this book is designed to help its readers take tests with more confidence and a greater chance of success. While the book should prove helpful in some ways even to experienced test-takers, it is intended primarily for people who feel nervous about taking tests. This is a very large group. It includes students who haven't done well on tests in the past; people who have been out of school for a few years and who must take a test for a job or a license; students who are planning to take tests for admission to college; and, finally, those who may be good at taking tests but who worry about everything. As I said, it's a large group.

How to Take a Test is the product of time and money and caring and the effort of many people. By recognizing the need for a book like this, and by providing the funds to make it possible, Educational Testing Service (ETS) has demonstrated its corporate capacity for caring in a sense that is both moral and personal. In its own way, *How to Take a Test* is an expression of ETS's confidence in the improvability of human performance in the complex world of modern education. For such generous support, the project director, the author, and the steering committee that got the book started, all members of the ETS staff, are proud and grateful.

Certain individual partners in this enterprise of book-writing must be mentioned by name:

Thelma L. Spencer was project director, which means that she managed and coordinated the whole enterprise from beginning to end, giving it force and focus and direction (in addition to keeping it on schedule).

Nathaniel H. Hartshorne was the first editor, meaning that he remanufactured early drafts and blended in the suggestions of a dozen critics in such subtle ways that the book reads as if it had but one author.

Sarah D. Sharp was the editor who carried the book through its final phases. The final copy is a tribute to her patience in handling the multitude of details connected with producing a book of this type.

The project was first proposed by *Arthur M. Kroll* who, being encouraged by ETS officers to suggest action, gathered about himself an ad hoc task force composed of Dr. Spencer, *Lena B. Brown, William U. Harris,* and *William C. Parker.* It was this ad hoc task force that breathed life into the project and served as a steering committee for the director over its whole duration.

The author's manuscript—many pages of bad typing fly-specked with the author's and editor's corrections—could not, of course, have reached a publisher without the efforts of a skilled typist. In this case, I was fortunate enough to have the benefit of two skilled and patient people: *Gloria M. Cain*, who typed and proofread the initial drafts, and *Marissa G. Burch*, who typed the final ones.

Other individuals, who will not be named but whose contributions made the project succeed, include the officers of ETS and the dozens of staff colleagues who took time in their busy lives to read and criticize drafts. Caring *can* be a group action.

Redington Beach, Florida   J.E.D.

SOME THINGS YOU NEED TO KNOW FIRST

- What a test is
- Purposes of tests
- Kinds of tests

Chapter 1

Chapter 1

SOME THINGS YOU NEED TO KNOW FIRST

If you're in school today, there's probably a test in your future—next year or next month or perhaps even tomorrow. It may be a test that a lot of people take to get into college, or a test for a job, or possibly a teacher-made test in math or history or Spanish. But it's there and it won't go away. You've got to get ready for it.

If you've always done well on tests, there's not much point in reading this book. You don't need any help. But if you haven't had much experience with tests and you don't know what to expect or how to prepare for one, or if you've done poorly on past tests and you feel you can't take them, this book is for you.

A test is a kind of job, and success on one nearly always depends on the experience you bring to it. If your experience and interests have been mostly in things outside the classroom—a job or work at home or a hobby—tests in school subjects may seem unfamiliar and perhaps unfair. That's probably because you've had one kind of experience and the test is aimed at people who have had another.

In this book, you'll find chapters on how to get ready for a test, things to remember at the test administration, procedures to follow when you take a multiple-choice test or an essay test, sample questions and explanations of the answers, some things to consider after you take the test, and descriptions of the scores you'll receive. In the back of this book, there's a section called "Test Talk" with a list of definitions and explanations of words, phrases, and directions you often find on tests (or in booklets about tests), and a sample test you can take for practice. Reading this book and using the material in

3

the back can give you experience that will help you feel better about tackling a test.

What a test is. Too many people think that a test is a device to trick you into showing your ignorance or to measure some trait that you'd rather not reveal. Those things are not true. You should look at every test as a way of demonstrating for yourself or somebody else the things you know, the skills you can apply, the problems you can solve, the work you can turn out in a given time, the accuracy of your work, and so on. The way you perform on a test gives your teacher an idea of how well you understand what's been going on in class; it gives a college admissions officer an idea of whether or not you can do work at the college level; and it gives an employer an idea of how well you can do a job. In other words, a test is a way of showing what you know and can do.

The quizzes and midterm tests and semester examinations that are made up by teachers or counselors and reproduced in your school by Ditto or Multigraph or Xerox or some other copier are called "teacher-made" tests. Standardized tests, on the other hand, are given to many people in many schools and jobs. The word "standardized" means that the same test has been given under the same conditions to large numbers of people, and that your performance on that test can be compared with theirs or with your own previous performance on it. Standardized tests are often "objective," meaning that the score you get on them does not depend on the subjective judgment of the scorer (as an essay grade does). Objective tests are scored by comparing your answers with those on an answer "key" or list. Of course, teacher-made tests can be objective, too.

Why people give tests. The general reason for all testing is that people want to find out more about you in order to make decisions about you:

- Your teacher wants to find out what things you've learned, what information you remember, what skills you're developing, what things you still need to learn.

- Your counselor wants to find out how you're getting along generally in school, what your strong points and weak points are, what your interests and skills are, what you have in mind for your own future.

- Admissions officers and counselors at colleges—people who don't know you—want to know how well you can do at school work compared with successful students at that college.

- Employment officers want to know how skillful you are in certain kinds of work so they can make a decision about hiring you.

There are many other reasons for giving tests, but these are the main ones. Testing specialists lump them under these three headings:

Guidance testing—to help you decide what to do next

Admissions testing—to show the admissions officer at a college or vocational school what you can do; usually consists of achievement tests (to find out what you've learned in subjects such as history or English) and aptitude tests (to find out about the general skills you have to apply to new learning situations)

Employment testing—to show an employer what you can do

Tests You Will Meet Most Often

There are many more tests in the world than there is room here to describe, but the ones you're most likely to encounter fall into five major classes:

Academic (ability and achievement) tests. This general type of test outnumbers all the other kinds combined. You will take academic tests all through your school and college years and on the job. A large number of tests in this category are called "ability" tests. It may surprise you to know that the IQ tests that people talk about so much ("What is your kid's IQ? My kid has the highest IQ in his class!") are just ability tests that have been given different names.

There are more than a hundred of this type of ability test, most of which have the words *ability* or *intelligence* or *aptitude* or *mental maturity* in their titles. Many of these tests are said to measure a trait called "intelligence" that remains pretty much unchanged throughout a person's life. This is simply not true. There is no test that measures how intelligent you are because intelligence involves too many things to be measured by one test. The best these tests can do is give you a selection of tasks or problems that are something like the tasks or problems you will face in school or on the job. If you do those tasks well, you are likely to do similar jobs well in school and at work. That's all there is to it.

The other most commonly used tests in the academic test category are achievement tests. Because we are talking about academic tests (meaning tests used mostly in schools), "achievement," as we use it here, refers to what you can do with questions in academic subjects like history and mathematics. There are literally hundreds of them in directories of standardized tests (tests that are given in exactly the same way to many people), and they are pretty much alike in what they are trying to get at, though they differ in the way they go about it. In Chapter 6, you'll see some of the kinds of questions that are used in achievement tests.

When you look at these test questions, you may wonder whether there is any real difference between ability tests and achievement tests. Actually, there's not much. Achievement tests generally cover what you've learned in school over a short period of time—say, a semester or a year—while ability tests tend to focus on certain basic skills in such things as reading or math, skills used in many different kinds of situations and ones you've learned in and out of school over a long period of time—about as many years as you've been in school.

Essay tests. On this kind of test, you write a paragraph or more in response to a question. This makes some people nervous. "*I* can't write," they say. Maybe they can't and maybe *you* can't either, but sometime soon you may have to take an essay test. If you know something about this kind of test, you'll have a head start when you take one. You'll find some useful information about preparing for essay tests as well as some strategies for taking them in later chapters.

Interest inventories. You don't need to prepare for or worry about interest inventories at all. They consist of questions that help you think about yourself—about what you like to do and what your interests may be for the future. There is no "best" score on an interest inventory, so there is no pressure to do well on the test. Some people may say that a high score in an occupational field means that you would be good or successful in that field. Inventories of this kind don't indicate this sort of information, and you shouldn't let anyone tell you that they do. So take these inventories as exercises that will help you find out more about yourself, not as some kind of test to be beaten.

Vocational aptitude tests. This is a special kind of test whose tasks are a lot like the kinds of work you do in real life for pay. Like all other tests, a vocational aptitude test measures your experience and skill in handling certain kinds of tasks. Some of them, especially the tests concerned with vocational aptitudes for office jobs and paper work, are like academic tests. Others, especially those that test your mechanical or dexterity skills, are quite different from tests you usually find in school.

When several vocational aptitude tests are given together in what's called a "battery," the results often give you and your counselor or employer some idea of what sorts of job skills you have developed and which ones you haven't developed. Vocational aptitude tests usually are interesting to take and, when they touch on some skills that you have already developed, they can be fun.

Performance tests. This kind of test requires you to demonstrate your ability by doing the actual job itself rather than answering questions about it. When you apply for a driver's license, for example, you must first pass a paper-and-pencil test of questions to demonstrate what you know about driving and safety and then a performance test to demonstrate how well you drive.

What about That Test You're Going to Take?

Now that you have a better idea of what a test is, why people give tests, and what some of the tests are that you'll meet most frequently, it's time to think about that test you're going to take next week or next month. How are you going to get ready for it? The next chapter should give you some ideas.

Chapter 2

FIND OUT ABOUT THE TEST AHEAD OF TIME

- Questions to ask
- Sources of information

Chapter 2

FIND OUT ABOUT THE TEST
AHEAD OF TIME

Football teams spend hours every week looking at movies of the next opponent they'll meet. Nobody asks why they do this; the reason is clear: They want to know what to expect so that they can plan for it. This is good strategy in football, and it's good strategy in test taking: Find out ahead of time what the test is like.

There are several sources of information about tests and what they're like. If you want to find out about a teacher-made test, you'll have to ask the teacher who made it. If the test you're about to take is a school or college or departmental test (made by many teachers), one or another of the teachers who are involved will be your best source; get information from several of them if you can. If it's a test given by the school system or the state, teachers may offer some help, but counselors are likely to be closer to this kind of information. If it's a test given by an outside agency, like the College Board, there's a lot of information and practice material you can get if you know whom to ask and where to write for it. This chapter will give you suggestions not only on what to ask but also where to get the information you need.

Starting below is a list of questions to ask about tests and some suggestions about where to find the answers.

Finding out about a test ahead of time—becoming familiar with different kinds of tests—will mean an important saving of time when you take the test and may help you do better than if you're uninformed and confused.

11

Questions to Ask Ahead of Time

What will the test cover? If you plan to prepare for the test, it's a good idea to know what to prepare *for*. If the words used to describe the test are "scholastic aptitude" or "academic ability" (or any combination of words that leads you to suspect that the test will attempt to measure your general ability to do school work), it will probably consist of questions that test your reading ability, your vocabulary, and your skill at solving math problems. Find out if the test includes questions on vocabulary, reading comprehension, and math, like those shown in Chapter 6 (What Tests Are Like).

If the test is to be an achievement test, it will measure your knowledge in a particular subject, and you should ask questions about the specific content of the test. What topics will it cover? For example, if the test is in history, what period of history? English history or American history? Will it concentrate on a short period of time like the Civil War or a longer period of time like the 200 years of exploration and settlement in this country? Will it consist mainly of questions asking for recall of facts? Or will it call for interpretation of facts given in the test?

If it's a math test, find out what levels or topics will be covered. At the level of the elementary grades, it will be the fundamental operations of addition, subtraction, division, and multiplication; at the high school level, it's likely to be general math, algebra, geometry, and calculus. Find out which ones will be emphasized.

If you find that the upcoming test is to measure your skill at doing something (like typing or shorthand or carpentry or auto mechanics or hairdressing or bookkeeping), ask: Will the test require me to show what I can do with a real assignment and with real materials and equipment in my hands? Or will it be a test in which I just have to answer printed questions about the job? This is a very important question to get answers to ahead of time. There's not much point in sharpening up your skill at operating a swing saw if the test is done with paper and pencil. On the other hand, if you find out that the test is to be a paper-and-pencil measure, you'll improve your chances of success by reviewing what the textbooks say about operating a swing saw.

The words to use in asking questions about this characteristic of an upcoming test are these two: Is it to be a *paper-and-pencil* test or will it be a *performance* test? Licensing exams in many trades are combinations of paper-and-pencil and performance tests, like the test for a driver's license described on page 7. The test for licensing beauticians in most states, for example, consists of several hours of questions you answer with paper and pencil followed by a performance test in which you demonstrate what you know by cutting, coloring, or styling hair, manicuring, and so on.

It pays to know what to expect—well ahead of time.

If you ask your questions in a friendly way, most teachers and counselors will do all they can to get information for you. If you're hostile about it, or if you just look as if you have a chip on your shoulder, people will be less likely to help you with information, especially if it requires work to get it. So go about your question-asking as diplomatically as you can. But remember, you have a right to ask the questions listed in this chapter, and the least you can expect from a teacher or counselor is some advice about where you can find the answers.

What kind of a test will it be? Will the test be all or mostly multiple-choice questions in which you choose the right answer from among four or five given answers? Is some of the test or all of it in the form of completion questions in which you finish a phrase or sentence by writing in your own answer? Is it an essay test, or does it have an essay section? Is it a test composed mostly of problems to be solved (in mathematics or science)? Does it require you to compute your answers or just choose the correct answer from among four or five given? Does it include maps or graphs to be interpreted?

How long will the test be? Does it come in just one section or in several short sections or subtests? Will there be rest breaks at any time during the test? How much will speed count? In other words, is the test timed so that nearly everyone will answer all the questions? If most of the students who take the test are not expected to finish it, speed is important, and you should take this into account when you take the test. In any case, it's important to be aware of how much time you have and to use it well.

How will you answer the questions? By blackening boxes on a separate answer sheet? By writing out your answers on the test itself? By writing answers on a separate sheet or in a booklet? By manipulating tools or materials while the examiner watches? By punching response keys on a computer terminal? By doing your work (computation, for example) on the test itself and then transferring your answers to a separate sheet?

If the test has an answer sheet, what kind is it? Have you used it before, enough to be comfortable with it? Some publishers of standardized tests make practice answer sheets available to counselors and teachers. Ask your teacher if there are practice materials available for the test you're about to take. If they are available, ask to see them. If the practice materials are not available, ask your teacher or counselor to find out about the answer sheet—how you code your name and blacken the boxes and other details. The answer sheets for standardized tests can be complicated, so you owe it to yourself to find out all you can about them before you take the test.

If the upcoming test has been made by your teacher or someone else in your school, either a teacher or a counselor can probably tell you exactly what the answer sheet is like. If it's complicated, they might even draw it on a chalkboard for you. They'll probably be glad to do this if you take the trouble to ask them.

None of this may seem very important, but if you start to take a test that requires you to use a strange device for answering questions, you could use up a good deal of valuable time trying to figure out how to code your name and answer the test questions. So be sure to ask about it.

How will the test be scored? On an essay test, of course, somebody will read what you've written. But who will that person be? Your teacher? A team of several teachers you know? One person you don't know? A team of people who are strangers to you? And how much emphasis will they put on each aspect of your essay? How many points will be given to the ideas in your essay, the organization and wording, and how many to mechanics—usage, punctuation, spelling, and handwriting?

On a multiple-choice test made by the teacher, the scoring undoubtedly will be done by the teacher using a hand-made list of correct answers. Here is where neatness counts; the teacher doing this work by hand soon becomes impatient if your answers are sloppy or marked in the wrong places or too faint to be read.

On any test for which you mark your answers on a separate answer sheet to be scored by a machine, there will be some special things to look out for. A scoring machine will not have any prejudice, either for you or against you, but it will penalize you for not following directions when you use the answer sheet. (There's more information on this in Chapter 5.)

Will there be penalties for guessing? Some teachers and test-makers try to discourage you from guessing on multiple-choice tests when you're not sure of the correct answer. One way they do this is to subtract points for wrong answers. Most of the time, if the penalties are not too heavy, it pays you to guess anyway. (For a further discussion of guessing, see Chapter 5.)

How much will handwriting and spelling count? If the test is to be a multiple-choice standardized test with a separate answer sheet, you won't be asked to write very much more than your name and address, but they must be written clearly. On essay and other kinds of written tests, it's hard to tell how important spelling and handwriting will be to the scorer unless you ask him or her. If you can't ask, it would be wise to assume that points would be taken off for messy handwriting and sloppy spelling and be as careful as you can while you're writing the test.

What supplies will you need when you take the test? Your own pencils? Scratch paper? Slide rule or hand calculator? Ruler for graphing work? Tools, if it is to be a performance test? In other words, what will you need to take into that test room besides yourself?

Any special gimmicks in the test? Some test-makers have an unusual way of presenting their tests. For example, a few standardized tests have pages that are cut so that an answer sheet bound into the back of the test book is revealed one column at a time as you move through the test. A few others have answer sheets that you punch holes in instead of marking with a pencil to show your answers. Some answer sheets are made so that you keep rubbing out covered answers until you uncover the right one (and your score depends on how many answers you rub out in the whole test—the fewer the better).

The answer sheets you should become familiar with before the test are those made to be scored by electronic machines; there are only a few kinds of these, so after you've taken some tests that use them, they will no longer seem gimmicky, if they ever did. Anything that's new and unfamiliar to you should be looked at, asked about, and, if possible, tried out before you meet it in the testing room.

Where to Get Answers to Your Questions

About teacher-made tests. This source is obvious. If your teacher made the test, your teacher should have the answers to your questions. The best time to ask is when the teacher tells you that there will be a test. In that way, you give the teacher a chance to answer your questions and those of others at the same time, and he or she doesn't have to repeat the answers for individual students.

Once in a great while, you may be surprised by a teacher who will not answer your questions because he or she is in a bad mood or is embarrassed because you asked your questions in a hostile way. If that happens, don't get uptight about it. Keep cool and go see the teacher alone after class and explain that you really are interested in doing your best job on the test and want to be sure that the test doesn't catch you unprepared in any way.

About school-wide or district-wide tests. These are the tests that are made somewhere in your school system but not by your teacher. Since most teachers want their students to show up well on any tests, particularly those made by somebody else, yours will probably be willing to help you with your questions. Again, it's best to ask your questions in a class session so that the teacher can gather all the questions and inform groups of students instead of just you alone.

About statewide tests. These are tests that have been built by people outside your school and district but that almost always are given (administered) in your own school by your teachers or counselors. Most of them are printed and look just like other standardized tests, although now and then you'll see one that's been duplicated from typewritten sheets. All of them (except for an occasional essay test) have separate answer sheets for electronic scoring, so you'll have a lot of questions to ask about a state test before it arrives. These will be the same questions you would ask about any standardized test, but the sources of the answers you get may be different. Start asking your questions as soon as you hear that the test is coming. Ask your teachers, your counselor, even your principal.

Sometimes state tests are made up by teachers from all over the state, acting under the direction of the department of education in your state capital, and sometimes they are made under contract by a professional agency somewhere else. In either case, the testing arrangements are nearly always made through the state department of education, which conducts training sessions for counselors and test coordinators all over the state. All information about the test and what it's like comes through these coordinators.

Most statewide testing programs provide test coordinators with elaborate descriptions of their tests and answer sheets, giving them instructions as if they were the students about to take the tests. So information about the tests does exist, usually right in your school, and is available to you. Many state testing programs provide printed descriptions of their tests and practice sheets to acquaint you with their answer sheets. Ask your teacher and counselor about these things. The coordinator may have them in his or her office and will distribute them to the teachers and counselors at the appropriate time.

About tests given for licensing, certification, and employment. Finding out about tests given by licensing agencies or employment offices for licensing or certification in a trade or profession is harder than finding out about tests given in school. If you're going to a beauty school, you can be sure that the people who run the school will know all about the licensing test in your state and will probably make a point of helping you to prepare for it. But if you've already been licensed in another state and just want to take the test without going to school first, you'll have a harder time getting information about the test from a beauty school. If you've been employed on a temporary basis in a shop until you get your license, you can ask the other beauticians what the test is like. Better yet, write to the licensing agency (usually in the state capital) and ask for all the information they can give you about the licensing test: what it's like, where it's given, when it's given, what you need to bring with you to the test, and so on.

The same procedure should be followed in whatever specialty you seek to enter, whether it be carpentry, plumbing, fitting eyeglasses, electrical work, or over-the-road truck driving. You have to go out and hunt up the information that will let you know in advance what the test is like. The sources of information are different in every state and different from field to field.

About tests given by outside agencies. Some of the tests best known to high school and college students are built, published, and administered all over the country by agencies that specialize in testing for admission to institutions and professions. The tests in this category are usually called "admission tests."

There are several major testing agencies whose tests are used in more admission-testing programs than any others. These agencies develop and administer tests under their own name or under contract to a group of schools or colleges or a professional organization. Educational Testing Service (ETS) develops and administers the Scholastic Aptitude Test (SAT) for the College Board. The American College Testing Program (ACT) develops and administers the ACT Assessment under the direction of its own board of trustees.

To get information about the test you'll be taking, ask your counselor or local librarian for the address of the testing agency that publishes it. Most agencies will send you a descriptive bulletin with sample questions. Sometimes, as with the College Board's SAT, they'll send you a whole test. You may even find that your counselor has some of these materials on hand.

HOW TO STUDY FOR A TEST

- Reviewing
- Cramming
- Preparing for an essay test
- Physical preparation

Chapter 3

HOW TO STUDY FOR A TEST

The ideal way to prepare for a test, of course, is to keep up with the reading and the discussion and the practice and the reviewing of fundamentals all through the year. But suppose you haven't stayed in shape and you need to do some fast catching up before the test. If you're like lots of people in school and college who do things that way, this chapter has been written for you. It contains ideas and suggestions on how to prepare for a test in an organized and systematic way.

Decide what to review. The first thing to do in preparing to take a test is to decide what to study. The first part of Chapter 2 made a special point of the need to find out ahead of time what the test will be like and what it will cover, and then gave some suggestions about how to find out. So read Chapter 2 again if any of this has slipped your mind. Once you have a good idea of what the test will be about, focus your preparation on those particular skills and that particular content and don't waste time on other things.

If you're going to take an ability or aptitude test like the College Board's Scholastic Aptitude Test (SAT) or the ACT Assessment, there are several things you can do to prepare for it. Read Chapters 4, 5, and 6 of this book so you'll have an idea of what to expect when you get to the test center, what multiple-choice test questions are like, and how to approach them. Then read the testing agency's booklet about the test (for example, *Taking the SAT*), which gives sample test questions.

The rest of this chapter is about studying for achievement tests in specific subjects such as history, math, or English.

Gather everything you've collected in the course—books, lecture notes, projects, and reports. Now add to this pile a set of your own rough notes on what *you* think the teacher thinks are the most important topics or issues or elements in the course. This set of notes about the teacher's priorities may be as important as anything else you have in that pile of material because it's very likely to reveal the topics to be emphasized in the test. If the test is an important one to the students, it's also an important one to the teacher, and since teachers are human beings, they tend consciously or unconsciously to put more emphasis in class on the topics you will be tested on later. So if you can locate in your memory and in your notes the things that the teacher has emphasized and concentrate on those things, you'll do well.

Now drive your detective work a little deeper. Try to recall exactly how the teacher developed the topic you've decided is worth reviewing. Did she emphasize remembering certain facts? Did he stress your skill in doing certain things? Did she emphasize your learning to *apply* the facts at your command or just to remember them? And so on. By putting together evidence of what the teacher thinks is most important in the area to be tested, you'll develop a preview of the test content. This is how your review starts. You're bringing your review into focus.

This job is usually easier and faster and more accurate if several people with different strengths—all of them about to take the same test—do the job of focusing together. They ask each other: "What do *you* think the teacher will put in the test? What makes you think so? Produce the evidence."

If you pay attention to what you're doing and take it seriously, one session of a couple of hours should be enough time for you to put together an outline of what needs to be covered in your review.

Once your plan of review has been brought into focus on things that are likely to be in the test, your next step should be to select those things in your outline that you know least about or are least sure of. (Do this by yourself.) Put these least-sure-of items at the top of your review list, giving them top importance, and put off to the last those things that you're fairly confident you know. Now you have a review plan focused on the likely content of the test, one that probably reflects the opinions of your teacher, and one in which the things you need most to review in detail are at the top of your list.

You'll be surprised to find that after you've done the things suggested in the paragraph above—sorting over your notes and then bringing them into a focus on what the test is likely to contain— you'll have accomplished a great deal of review already. You'll have refreshed your memory of what's in the course, what things the teacher thinks are important, what things the other students think are important, and what things you're fairly sure of without much further review.

Reviewing questions at the top of the list. What you do with the items at the top of your list depends on what they are. If they're nothing more than facts that need to be remembered, set them aside and absorb them later in a cram session, a special kind of review technique that's discussed on pages 24-26. If they're subjects you may be asked to write about in an essay, or reason with, or apply to problems, you'll want to follow this method of review:

1. For each topic at the top of your priority list, read your notes again carefully—both your class notes and your notes from reading. If you didn't take any notes on your reading, get out the text again and read the section headings and topic sentences for all those parts that are on your priority list. If you own the book, underline the section headings and topic sentences. (You won't go far wrong if you assume that the first sentence in every paragraph is its topic sentence.) Remember that you should underline only section headings and topic sentences and only those in the parts of the book that deal with your high-priority review ideas. (People who really know how to do this kind of review also copy down the main ideas in what they've underlined, but you may not have time to do that.)

2. For topics like math or science, the approach is a little different. First, go through all the work you've done during the semester or year—your homework and assigned projects and quiz papers— and make two piles of what you find: a pile of what you succeeded in learning and a pile of problems or assignments that you earned poor grades on—what you didn't learn. Then go through the stack of what you didn't learn and set aside everything that you are reasonably sure you *have* learned since you did that assignment. What you have left is a small collection of evidence that points to skills you haven't learned. These should be the object of your review.

3. At this point, you're ready to join your review group again. Take your sorted notes, your underlined books, and your stack of what you haven't learned and go with three or four other people who want to review for the same test to a place where you can talk together quietly for a few hours without interruption. In this review session, you each take turns asking the group to help you in clearing up a doubt or illustrating a solution to a problem or thinking of what questions the test might ask about your most important topics. In this session, you might give one of the better-prepared members of your review group some of your notes on a topic you are weak on, then ask him or her to ask you some questions on that topic, the kinds of questions that might be in the test. One such review session lasting two or three hours—if it is done seriously and the time is used well—should be enough to give you all the benefit you can get out of that kind of review. If you still have some doubts about your preparation on certain topics, go back to your sorted notes and your underlined text and go over them some more.

Cram with a plan. You've discussed the high-priority items, and now the only things you have left are facts, definitions, vocabulary, and other things you feel you will not be able to remember without making an extra effort to fix them in your memory. It's time to cram.

Too many people think that cramming has to be a late and bleary-eyed reading of what should have been read months ago. That's not cramming; that's foolishness. Cramming should be completed a day or two before the test. (If you haven't done this, you'd be better off on the night before the test spending an hour or two in a rap session like the one mentioned earlier in this chapter; then get to bed in time for a good night's sleep.)

Cramming only works with items of factual recall—names, places, dates, spelling, formulas, codes, rules, regulations—things that are clear, not subject to debate, and usually expressed in short answers. Here's how to do it:

1. Make yourself a handful of paper slips, each about one-fourth the size of a sheet of notebook paper. (Cut them instead of tearing them so that they have smooth edges and can be shuffled easily.)

2. Starting with the first fact or date or other item you want to etch into your memory, write a very short question about it—then the answer. Like this:

What year did Columbus discover America?   1492

What country colonized Mexico?   SPAIN

Who appoints members of the U.S. Supreme Court?
   THE PRESIDENT

Who has the constitutional power to control education in this
   country?   THE STATES

What is the chemical formula of water? H_2O

What general led the British in the Battle of Waterloo?
   WELLINGTON

Where was Napoleon finally exiled?   ST. HELENA

Who was president of the Confederate States of America?
   JEFFERSON DAVIS

The name given to the first ten amendments to the
   Constitution is?   THE BILL OF RIGHTS

This pile of individual questions and answers is your set of cram
cards. Now you're ready for the cramming itself (although just by
the act of writing questions and answers you have already done a lot
toward memorizing your material).

3. Sit down with your set of cram cards and read each one aloud to
   yourself—first the question and then the answer.

4. Just reading questions and answers aloud gets dull after a couple
   of passes through the deck, so after the second or third pass, *draw
   a circle* around the answer to each question as you read it. On the
   next pass, draw a square or a rectangle as you read it. The reading aloud and the drawing around, or otherwise marking the answer, help you memorize much faster.

5. Next, ask somebody else to go through the deck with you, reading
   the questions while you respond. Instruct your reader to give you
   only a second or two to come up with the answers; if you fumble
   or hesitate or give a wrong answer, he should read the right answer aloud and go on to the next question. Keep repeating this
   procedure through your whole deck until you're tired of it or until you think you've memorized all the answers.

6. Now vary the procedure a little by having your partner give you
   the card each time you give a correct answer. Continue this way
   until you have all the cards.

7. Periodically go through the deck yourself, asking yourself only those questions you still can't answer quickly and correctly and once in a while sneak in some others. Shuffle your deck each time you go through it so that questions never come up in the same order.

8. Sometime on the day before the test (not the night before, if you can avoid it), go through the whole deck again a couple of times. Draw a circle or square around each answer as you read it. Then close your eyes and repeat each answer and try to see both the question and the answer in your mind.

That's cramming at its best. Accept no substitutes.

Cram cards are not crib cards. This is a warning that's important enough to rate a section all by itself. It probably occurs to most people that it would be helpful to take into the testing room a set of very small cards on which you've written the answers or facts that are especially hard to remember. These are called crib cards. Using them is called "cribbing" and is considered a serious violation of the rules of testing. So don't use crib cards or any other form of information smuggling. You're reading this book in an effort to increase your chances of success on a test; crib cards or other tricks that amount to cheating multiply your chances of failure. (For more information on this subject, see the section on cheating in the next chapter.)

What about cram books and coaching courses? If you're planning to take a test for entrance to college, you've probably wondered about those ads for cram books and courses that help you prepare for these tests. One important thing to keep in mind is that the people who publish these books and teach these courses and write these ads don't know you or your situation in school or how much you really need their special kind of help. There may be courses like theirs right in your school. So before you decide to spend your time and money on cram books or courses, get some advice from a teacher or counselor or someone else who does know you, who knows something about getting into college, and whose opinion you respect.

You'll find when you talk to your teacher or counselor that there are many questions to be asked before you make a decision about taking a coaching course or using a cram book. What materials and practices are used? How much will it cost in time and money? What effect will it have on your attitude as well as your test scores?

Since college entrance tests measure abilities that are acquired gradually over many years both in school and outside of school, it's not likely that your skills would improve very much during a short period of coaching. An important question, then, is whether the coaching would be of high enough quality and continued long enough to improve your scores more than they would improve anyway through your usual everyday learning experiences both in school and elsewhere.

Finally, it's important to understand that different people probably learn in different ways, so coaching and cram books may not have the same effect for you as they do for another student.

Preparing for an essay test. If the essay test is to be one made by your teacher, find out from other students what that teacher's favorite essay topics are. Many teachers keep the same list of topics or questions for years. Some teachers will even give you the questions in their list and tell you that only six of them will turn up in the test. It's perfectly legitimate to ask about what teachers prefer in essay questions, and it's usually not hard to find answers. Knowing in general what you're going to be asked to write about is an important advantage. Don't miss it.

If the essay test is to be one given by the school district or the state or some outside agency, ask your teacher to help you or the class find out what kinds of topics or questions are used. As mentioned earlier, if you're to take a test given by somebody else, your teacher is likely to be just as eager as you are for you to succeed. The teacher may have some observations about topics and questions that have been in the test in the past. The chances are very slight that this year's test will have exactly the same questions as it had last year, but the chances are good that they'll be the same *kinds* of questions.

If you know that you've got to face an essay test and you're not sure about how well you write complete sentences, go get some help from your teacher or someone in your class who knows how.

A special word of warning. Someday, when you have a very important test coming up, someone may offer to sell you a copy of the test ahead of time. What such people usually do is borrow or steal some test on the same subject out of a college library (a test that probably bears no resemblance whatever to the test you're going to take) and make copies of it.

Buying one of those tests is like spending your money on a wristwatch that some person on the street offers as "hot merchandise" but won't let you hold to hear if it ticks. More important, it's dishonest.

Prepare yourself physically too. What you feel like physically on the day of the test is crucial to success on any test. Here are some important points to remember.

- Get a good night's sleep.

- Stay away from stimulants. You may think that lots of black coffee or even some drugs will give you a "high" that will help you to be extra sharp. Actually, stimulants can make you so wide awake and hyped up that you miss the point on most of the test questions.

- Stay away from tranquilizers. If you follow all the other directions you've been given in this chapter, you won't need any artificial aid in soothing your nerves just before the test. It's better to be nervous than to fall asleep. A little anxiety before a test may be a good thing.

- Don't drink a lot of liquids before a test. Having to go to the rest room several times during the test will slow you down and disturb your trend of thought about the test.

- Don't eat a big meal just before going to the test. If you feel you need nourishment before the test, eat a snack, not a meal.

- If the test is the first thing in the morning, set your alarm to give you at least a full hour of lead time and get there early.

A final word. If you've prepared yourself well with an early review and if you've avoided all the things that would handicap you physically, you're ready for the test.

Chapter 4

IN THE TEST ROOM

- Concentrating on the test
- Asking questions
- How to complain

Chapter 4

IN THE TEST ROOM

While you're on your way to take a test, think about the common-sense advice in this chapter. It applies to any testing situation.

Give the test your complete attention. Remind yourself that this one period, however long it may be, has been set aside for you to demonstrate what you can do. All plans for other activities, all memories of past activities, all friends and foes, all problems and pleasures need to be blocked out of your mind. This kind of concentration is an important part of the skill you're being tested on.

Choose a good seat. In some of the test administrations you'll experience, you may be assigned a seat in a test center. But in other test situations, you may be able to choose your seat. That's important. Sitting in one place for a couple of hours, on a hard chair, can be difficult and tiring, so choose a seat that gives you enough leg room, good light, and is away from any open window that could distract you. It's especially important to choose a seat as far as possible from your friends. Friends are great, and everybody needs them, but they can be a hazard in a testing room where you are tempted to whisper humorous comments about certain questions or signal how far along you are or pantomime your appreciation of the girl or guy in the front row.

If you're left-handed, get there early and tell the examiner that you would prefer to have a seat with a left-handed writing board, if they have some. Keep remembering that in choosing your seat you are selecting the best possible spot in which to show your stuff on the test. Give yourself every break.

Do your talking some other time. Most people get nervous when they're about to take a test. And many people get talkative when they're nervous. Try to resist the impulse to be loud and funny just to relieve your tension. Use that time to think about the material you've learned.

Listen carefully. If you have a separate answer sheet, look at it as the examiner reads the directions for using it. Don't read ahead, because you may miss something important.

Read and listen to the directions on how to take the test and mark your answers. Don't think that all this is old stuff and that you don't need to read or listen. That could be a serious mistake. If you don't hear or don't understand the directions, ask the examiner to repeat them. (At the end of the directions, most examiners stop and ask: "Are there any questions?" That's the time to raise your hand and get your question answered or the directions repeated.) Too many students are embarrassed to say they have not understood and then have to push ahead in the test without knowing what they are doing. If you are to demonstrate your skill on anything, you have a right— and a duty to yourself—to know exactly what you're supposed to do and how you're supposed to do it. Don't let them start the test until you're sure that you have the directions straight. And don't ask your neighbor about them; ask the examiner. That's why examiners are there.

How to ask a question during the test. If you have a question about how to proceed while you are taking the test, raise your hand high enough to be seen, and the examiner will come over to you. Explain your problem in a whisper. The examiner is not allowed to help you answer a question or solve a problem that is part of the test, but sometimes he or she is allowed to help you understand what the question means or what a problem requires in the way of a solution.

How to complain. If you feel you have good cause for complaint (if the examiner won't repeat the directions or is impatient or hostile, if there's a distracting noise, if the lighting is poor, or some other problem), you should know what to do.

The first thing to remember (and the most important) is that you can complain later. If you feel you have a legitimate complaint and that it's worth arguing about, you'll have to be the judge of how long to argue and when to stop. When you reach that point, instead of blowing your top and the whole test with it, give in quietly and try to do the best you can on the test. Just keep your mind on the fact that you can complain later.

How you complain later depends somewhat on the kind of test it is, who's giving it, and for what purpose. If it's a test in a course given by your teacher, and the test has been made and given by that teacher, you may have a special problem on your hands. A procedure that usually works in this situation is to go to the teacher after the test and—as tactfully and nonaggressively as you can—review the whole incident with him or her. It's best to wait a while before doing this, to give tempers time to cool, and then to approach the teacher as if you both had a little misunderstanding to straighten out. Again, play it in a calm way; you don't get anywhere in the school world or most other places by making threats. If you and the teacher can't work out a reasonable solution, break off the discussion without losing your temper and make an appointment to see the principal or the dean. Then tell the principal or dean what happened as fairly and accurately as you can and suggest that your performance on that test should be considered in light of the problem you had in taking it. Again, keep your cool!

If the test was made up by the county or the school system or the state, you should take your gripe to your counselor or dean or to your teacher—depending on where you are likely to find a sympathetic ear. With this kind of problem, it always helps to find out if other students have the same gripe. Get them to join you in a group protest—low key, of course—in the counselor's or dean's office.

If the test is one that was given by a testing agency—say, one of the College Board tests or the American College Testing Program tests—or a state licensing agency, you should report any problems to the supervisor at the test center, who will file a report with the testing agency, or you can write out your complaint and send it directly to the agency. Your complaint will get more attention if it comes from you and several others who took the test and if you're specific and describe the circumstances as completely as you can. It's also a good idea to file your complaint right away instead of waiting until you get your scores. If your problem is serious enough, the agency may arrange for you to take the test again.

A word about cheating. There must be hundreds of ways to cheat on a test, ways that were invented years ago and have been tried each year since. Teachers and others who make and give tests have learned just what to look for to prevent cheating and to catch cheaters. On the College Boards, the ACT test, on licensing examinations given by the states, and other tests given to large numbers of people, the security measures used to keep students honest are surprising; most students wouldn't believe the efforts that are made by testing agencies to prevent cheating. Getting caught cheating on a test like this is worse than failing to show up for it. It may result in being rejected by the very college or profession that required you to take the test. Cheating on any test—big or small—is a serious violation and is not worth the risk.

Chapter 5

TEST-TAKING STRATEGIES

- Coding answer sheets
- Timing and pacing
- Guessing
- Taking essay tests

Chapter 5

TEST-TAKING STRATEGIES

Strategies for Taking Multiple-Choice Tests

By far the greatest number of important tests you take in your career will be wholly or partly multiple-choice, meaning that you must choose one of several possible answers for each question or problem.

Making a good multiple-choice test is not a simple matter. At major testing agencies such as Educational Testing Service, test committees, usually made up of teachers or college professors, and many test-making specialists work together for many months, sometimes more than a year, to make a test. Their job is to make sure that each question measures what it's supposed to measure, that the question itself has only one meaning, that there is only one right answer, and that the question is unbiased and is appropriate for the people who are being tested.

Schools and employers have used multiple-choice tests for many years, and a good deal of knowledge has been accumulated about how to take these tests and do well on them. This section describes some special features of multiple-choice tests and some techniques for taking them. Chapter 6 gives some sample questions that will illustrate what you read here.

Learning to cope with a scoring machine. Nearly all multiple-choice tests these days are scored by an electric or electronic machine. You can tell which kind will score your tests: If you have to use a special

37

pencil on the answer sheet and make all your marks heavy and black, your answer sheet will be scored by an *electric* machine that runs tiny amounts of electricity through your pencil marks. If you're allowed to use your own pencil on an answer sheet, the chances are good that the scoring will be done by an *electronic* machine that "looks" at your answer sheet with an optical scanner and can read your name if it is coded in a special grid on your answer sheet. The answer sheet that's used with an electronic scoring machine is the kind you'll see most often. Here's how you use it:

Once you've taken your seat in the test room and have received your test materials, you'll be instructed to turn first to your answer sheet, which will probably look a lot like the one on pages 115 and 116 in this book. This looks worse than it really is. The boxes that may look confusing are for coding your name and other identification so that the machine can "read" it. (The machine doesn't read any letter, of course, but records its location on the answer sheet.) Once you see that, things begin to clear up.

As the directions say, you are to print your name and address, the number of the center where you'll take the test, and the date you're going to take the test in box number 1. In box number 2, print the first four letters of your last name and your first and middle initials in the squares at the top of the box; then below the letter written in each square, you blacken the little oval or "bubble" that has that letter in it (see the illustration on page 39). Now, in the same way, code your date of birth, your sex, and your registration number, if you have one, in the spaces for this information. Most answer sheets want more than just this information about you—like the grade you're in, the college you want scores sent to, your student number, and so on—but it's all coded in exactly the same way.

Important: If you still don't understand how to code your name on the answer sheet, look up at your counselor or teacher right away and ask for some help.

When you have coded your name and other information, the test supervisor will give you directions about marking your answers to the test questions. Listen closely.

Every answer sheet of this type requires you to make a heavy pencil mark that just fills in a little circle, an oval, a square, a rectangle, or a pair of parallel lines. It's important that you make your mark very black and make it fill the whole space without spilling over. Neatness is very important. If you change your mind and mark a second answer and fail to erase your first answer completely, the machine may read your first answer and your second answer, conclude

**USE ONLY A SOFT LEAD PENCIL (NO. 2) FOR COMPLETING THIS ANSWER SHEET.
DO NOT USE INK OR BALL-POINT PEN.**

1.

YOUR NAME: _SMITH   JOHN   E_
(PRINT)   LAST   FIRST   MIDDLE

HOME ADDRESS: _1947   CENTER   ST._
(PRINT)   NUMBER AND STREET

EVANSTON   NJ   08540
CITY   STATE   ZIP CODE

CENTER: _TRENTON   745_
(PRINT)   CITY   NUMBER

DATE OF TESTING: _6 / 10 / 80_
MONTH   DAY   YEAR

---

2. YOUR NAME

FIRST 4 LETTERS OF LAST NAME				F.I.	M.I.
S	M	I	T	J	E

3. DATE OF BIRTH

MONTH	DAY	YEAR
JAN.	1 8	6 3

4. SEX

MALE ●

FEMALE ○

5. REGISTRATION NUMBER

| 3 | 4 | 2 | 5 | 1 | 4 | 6 |

that you have given two answers, and give you no credit. So the examiner isn't being fussy when he or she tells you about marking your answer sheet: the directions mean exactly what they say.

When the directions warn you to "Avoid making any stray marks on your answer sheet," you'd better believe that, too. Some people doodle on answer sheets and cause the scoring machine all sorts of grief. There's no way of knowing how the machine will handle these stray marks. It can be set to take a point off for doodles or for what seems to be two answers to the same question. So if your stray marks look like answers, you may be penalized. To protect yourself, erase completely.

While we're on the subject of marks on a machine-scored answer sheet, you should know that you can't write a message on an answer sheet and expect someone to see it. Even marking a big X through your answers won't do the trick. If you want something special done with your answer sheet (for example, if you don't want it scored), you must tell the person in charge of the test.

Be sure you know whether there is a penalty for guessing. If the examiner does not offer any information about guessing, ask. If the answer is that your score will consist of the total number of right answers you get, that means there is *no* penalty for guessing. If the examiner says only: "There is a penalty for guessing" or "Your score will be reduced for wrong answers," ask him or her how large the penalty or the reduction will be.

Time yourself. It's a good idea to bring a watch because the testing room may not have a clock. Be sure that you know how much time you have for the test or for each timed section of the test. On some tests, you're not allowed to go back and check your work on sections that have been completed, so timing yourself through the test is very important.

When the test begins. When you're ready to go and the signal to begin is given, open your test and position it in a good place by your answer sheet. Make a mental note of what the time will be when you'll have five minutes left to review your work, and then proceed like this:

1. Starting with the first question or problem, read the problem or reading passage that constitutes the question all the way through and then read carefully all the answer choices for each test question. It's a mistake to think that because the first or second an-

swer choice looks good to you, you don't need to read the other four or five. You lose points that way because sometimes there is another choice that answers the question more precisely. Or you may find something in one of the later choices that will suggest to you that you misunderstood the question. So read all the answers before you choose one.

2. Don't puzzle more than a few seconds over any question or problem. If you don't know the answer immediately, go on to the next question. If you do skip a question, however, be sure you also skip the corresponding answer space for that question on your answer sheet. On your first pass, go through the whole test this way, marking answers only to those questions you're sure of. On the other hand, don't work so fast that you haven't given yourself any time to think about a question. That's wasteful, too. The idea is to pace yourself. Keep moving so that you'll have time to consider all questions at least once and some more than once.

3. On your second pass through the test, try the questions you couldn't answer easily the first time. Now you should change your attack slightly. Read each of these questions or problems again and all the answer choices to see if you can eliminate some of them.

   Suppose you've eliminated three of the five possible responses, but you're totally in the dark about which of the remaining two is the right answer. This is the time to use whatever *hunch* you have—where there is just a choice between two possibilities. For example, consider this question from the College Board *PSAT/ NMSQT Student Bulletin:*

> **Each question below consists of a word in capital letters, followed by five lettered words or phrases. Choose the word or phrase that is most nearly *opposite* in meaning to the word in capital letters. Since some of the questions require you to distinguish fine shades of meaning, consider all the choices before deciding which is best.**
>
> PINNACLE: **(A)** buttress **(B)** hinge **(C)** abyss
> **(D)** surface **(E)** oblivion

Let's say that you know that *pinnacle* means a peak, or the highest point of something. Then let's say you're able to eliminate *buttress, hinge,* and *oblivion,* which have nothing to do with peaks or high points. That means you have to decide between *surface* and *abyss,* but you don't know which is the right answer.

In this situation, you'd look at the question again. It asks you to choose the word or phrase that is "most nearly *opposite*" in meaning to *pinnacle*. You may not know the exact meaning of *surface*, but you know it has something to do with being on the ground. That's different from a peak or the highest point of something. But is it more different, or more nearly opposite, than *abyss*? Let's say you're not sure how to define *abyss*, but you have a hunch that it has something to do with a pit or a hole or something deep. A pit or a hole or something deep would be farther into the ground than *surface* and therefore more nearly opposite in meaning to a peak or *pinnacle*. So you'd choose *abyss*, or choice (C). And you'd be right.

When and how to guess. A warning that there's a penalty for guessing is given to discourage you from trying to improve your score by guessing blindly. The cautious test-taker guesses very carefully. If there's no penalty for guessing (if only correct answers are counted), then obviously you'd be wise to guess.

When there is a penalty, it's important for you to understand how guessing can affect your score and to use guessing strategies that can work to your advantage. The first thing you should do is find out whether you know anything at all about the question that is being asked. If you do know something, you'll probably be able to spot one or two wrong answer choices. Then you can decide whether or not to guess among the rest of the answers.

Your chances of choosing the correct answer increase, of course, with every choice you can eliminate. For example, on a five-choice test, if you can reduce your choices to four, you'll raise your chances of getting the right answer from 20 to 25 percent. If you can reduce the choices to three, your chances of choosing the right answer will increase to 33⅓ percent, and if you can reduce the choices to two, your chances of getting the right answer are then even at 50-50.

An example might help show you how important having a guessing strategy can be. Suppose you're taking a multiple-choice test that has 100 questions, each with five answer choices, and there's a penalty for guessing. You answer 60 and skip 40 because you know little or nothing about their content. You get all of the 60 right, so your raw score is 60, and nothing is taken off because you didn't try to answer the other 40 questions. Because you have a strategy for guessing, you don't have to settle for the score of 60, even if there's a guessing penalty, because you know that by using the strategy of eliminating two or three answers that seem wrong and guessing at the two or three that are left, you're bound to pick up some more points. The odds are in your favor.

You answer the remaining 40 questions, and you get, say, half of them right and half of them wrong. The 20 right answers are added to your raw score of 60 $(60 + 20 = 80)$. The 20 wrong answers are then scored using the guessing penalty—20 wrong answers divided by the penalty of ¼ point for every wrong answer $(20 \div \frac{1}{4} = 5)$. Five points subtracted from your score of 80 gives you a total raw score of 75, which is much better than the 60 you'd have been forced to settle for if you hadn't used your guessing strategy.

The same kind of scoring would be used for a test that had four-choice questions. You'd get one point for every question you answered correctly, zero for every question you skipped, and you'd lose ⅓ point for every question you answered incorrectly. So, no matter how many answer choices a test has, it's almost always a good idea to guess if you have a good strategy.

Strategies for Taking Essay Tests

Taking an essay test is an entirely different procedure from taking a multiple-choice test. The most obvious difference, of course, is that you have no answers to choose from; you have a question, or several questions, and a blank sheet of paper. You create your own answer(s). This calls for planning as well as writing.

Most essay tests require you to write two to four short essays on different subjects or in answer to different questions. Some essay tests will contain a lot of questions and ask you to write only a sentence or two in response to each. Occasionally, you'll meet one in which you're asked to write a long composition on just one topic.

The essays you write may be in tests for admission to college, in tests for employment, even in tests for promotion on the job or in the armed services. Probably not all the people who look at them will be English teachers, but they usually will pay attention to grammar, spelling, and all the things English teachers pay attention to. So go into the essay test as if your job were to please the toughest and fussiest teacher of English you ever had.

Sometimes the directions for essay tests seem to be short on information and long on confusion. They use words like *discuss, compare, list,* and so on. Or you are expected to *analyze* a given situation even if the word *analyze* is not used, as in this example:

> **Give at least three reasons why the U.S. Senate rejected President Woodrow Wilson's proposal that the United States become a member of the League of Nations.**

Here are definitions of some of the words used in essay tests and examples of questions using the exact words or being put in such a way that you must answer in a certain way.

compare: to examine the character or qualities of, especially in order to show resemblances or differences

> **Compare the principles of the League of Nations with those of the United Nations in the area of human rights.**

classify: to assign to a category

> **Give the names of six Third World nations and identify one major problem they have in common.**

evaluate: to make a value judgment and support it with evidence

> **The word "evil" has been used to describe the character Iago in *Othello*. Define evil and give three instances of Iago's behavior that fit the description.**

summarize: to cover the main points briefly and concisely

> **State the plot of the opera *Tristan and Isolde* by Wagner.**

Some other words you will meet in essay tests are given below. Look up the definitions of these words in your dictionary. You might also ask your teacher to show you how each of these words is translated into action. Once you begin to feel at home with words like these, you'll find they can help you show how much you know when you take an essay test.

apply	distinguish	interpolate	state
associate	develop	interpret	show
arrange	derive	list	synthesize
assess	document	match	support
break down	explain	outline	trace
construct	examine	organize	translate
contrast	formulate	paraphrase	test
compile	generalize	predict	validate
criticize	group	relate	verify
demonstrate	indicate	rank	
discuss	illustrate	select	

Before you begin the test, be certain that you know how much time you'll be allowed for each section (if the test has sections) or for the whole test. Find out, too, how much each section counts toward the total score. When you have enough information and have received your essay assignments, follow this procedure:

1. Read all of the questions or topics carefully. If you have to choose from a list of topics or questions, do your choosing before you

write anything. Think about each one for a minute before deciding. Choose topics on which you can write clearly and knowledgeably, not topics on which you think you can throw out the greatest number of words.

2. Working fast, briefly outline on a separate piece of paper (or on the back of the test booklet) the main ideas that come to your mind first when you think of each of the chosen topics. (This is important for most people because after you've been writing on Topic 1 for a while, you may forget several of the good ideas you had for Topic 2.) These are only notes to yourself, so they can be just fragments of sentences, often single words, to help remind you of what you first thought of when you saw the topic. Do this for all the topics you've decided to write about.

3. When you're ready to begin writing, start with the topic that appears first on the list and indicate that you're writing about that topic. (It helps the grader of your test to know at the outset which topic you're writing about.)

4. Figure out how much time you can devote to each topic. By dividing the number of minutes allowed for the whole test by the number of topics you must write about, you'll know roughly how much time you can give to each. Then allow some time before the end of the test to read over what you've written. (If the test is 50 minutes long and you must write on three topics, you have 15 minutes for each plus 5 minutes for checking your work.)

Allocate about one-third of your time for each topic to planning what you're going to write and two-thirds to actual writing. Of that 15 minutes to be devoted to Topic 1, then, you would spend about 5 minutes in planning what you're going to say and about 10 minutes in actually writing it. All this sounds more complicated than it really is; you can do the whole business of dividing up your test time in a matter of seconds. But be sure to do it so you won't run out of time just when you've been inspired and are writing furiously.

If more than one paragraph is required for each topic, use your notes to pick out the most important few ideas to build paragraphs on. If the test asks for only one paragraph on the topic, decide what your most important idea is.

You're now ready to start writing.

5. Organize each paragraph this way: The first sentence is the topic sentence and should state the major point of the paragraph. The

next sentence should contain the strongest evidence, the clearest explanation, or the best logic you can think of to support the topic sentence. If there are other things you want to say in support of what you said in your topic sentence, put them in the order of their importance (ending with the least important) in succeeding sentences. If you include many supporting sentences in your paragraph, add one at the end that summarizes what you've said.

Each paragraph you write should be about one topic. If you go on to another, start a new paragraph, organizing it around your second topic sentence. Keep your paragraphs brief but informative.

Somebody has to read your writing in order to grade your essay test, so write clearly and neatly enough for that person to read your writing.

Write in complete sentences. Each sentence has to have a subject and a predicate. (The "stream of consciousness" style is not popular among essay-test graders.) Avoid long and complicated sentences.

Try always to use words that you know how to spell. English teachers sometimes put as much value on correct spelling as they put on complete sentences. If you don't know how to spell a word that expresses what you want to say, however, spell the word as best as you can and move on.

Try to work up an interest in what you're writing. If you keep thinking how bored you are by the essay topic, your feeling may show in your writing and slow up your flow of ideas.

Be sure to read over everything you've written before handing in your essays. Look to see that you've written complete sentences and punctuated them correctly and answered the questions completely.

What to do if you don't know the answers. If you think you know nothing about an essay question, the first thing to do is to stay calm. You probably know something about it. The next thing to do is to organize whatever you do know and present it in the best possible way. If you have an idea or an opinion about a topic and know a fact or two (even though they may not be the answers to the question), put them into a short and complete sentence or two that expresses that idea or opinion clearly and logically. If you don't have enough information to write a few sentences, try writing your answer in the form of an outline, using the essay question as your topic sentence and whatever facts or fragments of information you have as subtopics under it. Whatever you do, don't skip over an essay question because you think you don't know the answer. Most essay readers will give you some credit for a well-thought-out answer or part of an answer, even if it's not exactly what was called for.

These are some useful strategies for taking any multiple-choice or essay test. In the next chapter, we'll take a close look at the kinds of questions you'll find in the tests themselves.

Chapter 6

WHAT TESTS ARE LIKE

This chapter should give you an idea of what you can expect to find in tests and how testing techniques differ from subject to subject. There are sample questions included for you to study and try so that when you come across similar question types in a real test, you won't have to waste time wondering what they're all about.

Most of these sample questions are of average difficulty for high school students who have recently taken a course in the subject tested, but a few of them are difficult even for those students. So if you've taken no more than ninth grade general math, don't be discouraged if you trip over a problem in trigonometry.

Verbal Skills

Education of all kinds, particularly academic education in high schools and colleges, requires a high level of skill in language. Employment in skilled and supervisory occupations requires competence in communication, as does active citizenship. For this reason, testing used for school and employment purposes is more heavily loaded with measures of your skill in communicating—reading, writing, listening, and interpreting—than any other kinds of measures. (There are very few tests of your ability to communicate by speaking because of the mechanical difficulties of testing speech. Your skill in speaking is most likely to be judged on the basis of interviews or testimony by people who know you.)

Tests of reading comprehension. Do you understand what you read? Can you get the general drift of a paragraph by reading it just once? Do you remember details? Can you *interpret* what you read? (That is, can you figure out what authors are driving at, what their purposes might be, how they intend to achieve their purposes?) Can you criticize what you read, both as to its content and its logic?

All of these things are covered in good tests of reading comprehension. Look at the following sample questions taken from Sequential Tests of Educational Progress (original series) and see if you can figure out what the test-maker is trying to measure. The key to the correct answers is on page 64.

(1)   A flash of bright blue in the green depths of the piney woods caught the eye of wildlife biologist Hilbert Siegler of the Texas Game Commission. Then a second spot of blue stirred, as another jay sailed on silent wings to the same branch. The newcomer, holding a morsel of food in its beak, hopped closer to the first bird. Turning eagerly, the first jay lifted its crested head and accepted hungrily the gift its visitor poked down into its throat.

(2)   Siegler was astonished. In fledging season, young birds often continue coaxing food from their parents even after they have grown up; in courting season, bird swains often bestow dainties upon the females they are wooing. But this wasn't the season for fledglings, nor was it courting time. This was the dead of winter.

(3)   Hastily the wildlife expert raised his binoculars and got the answer. The recipient of the bounty was an adult jay, a grizzled veteran. The lower mandible of its beak had been broken off nearly at the base. It had no way to pick up food.

(4)   This impulse to share and cooperate is familiarly awakened in creatures of the wild by members of their immediate families. But here seemed to be something close to the human ideal of sharing.

(5)   Nature's creatures often exhibit impulses of self-assertion and competition. But all through life's vast range, these instincts are balanced by another kind of drive. Nature does not implant in her children just the single message: "Take care of yourself." There is a second ancient and universal injunction: "Get together." It is as vital as the breath of life.

(1) What kind of blue jay was fed?

   (A) A fledgling
   (B) An old blue jay, too weak to hunt his own food
   (C) An injured adult blue jay
   (D) A courted female

(2) **The author does** NOT **state**

    (E) who the wildlife biologist is
    (F) how the bird was injured
    (G) what the jay's injury is
    (H) what time of year it is

(3) **Which of the following titles is most appropriate?**

    (A) "Animals Help Each Other"
    (B) "Blue Jays in Winter"
    (C) "A Walk in the Woods"
    (D) "Feeding Birds Throughout the Year"

(4) **The author supports his main idea by**

    (E) citing an example
    (F) comparing different animals
    (G) showing cause and effect
    (H) quoting more than one authority

(5) **Paragraph 4 suggests that the author**

    (A) disapproves of the behavior he described in paragraph 1
    (B) thinks blue jays have little regard for each other
    (C) regards most interpretations of animal behavior with suspicion
    (D) admires what Hilbert Siegler saw

Reading comprehension tests differ so much that there can't be any general rule of thumb for approaching them. What many test-wise people do, however, is to quickly skim the questions before reading the passage. If the questions about the passage are short and if you can understand what they're asking without having to read all the answer choices, this may be a good technique for you. You lose a little time in skimming the questions first, but usually you can make it up by knowing what to look for as you read the passage.

This skim-the-questions-first method should work fairly well on questions like those above because the questions and answer choices are brief enough to be skimmed quickly. You might try this technique on the sample reading comprehension questions in a booklet such as the College Board's *Taking the* SAT. If you're good at skimming, this technique may be helpful to you.

On the other hand, the best method for you may be simply to read straight through the passage at your usual reading speed and then answer the questions, referring quickly back to the passage if you have to. Or it may work for you to read very quickly through the passage, look at the questions, and then read the passage more slowly. You decide what works best for you.

Generally, you can expect that with each reading comprehension passage you'll be asked questions that have to do with:

- What the passage is about (the subject of the passage and the points the author makes about it. You can often find the theme of a passage in the first, or topic, sentence of each of its paragraphs.)

- The details that support the subject (specific facts that help illustrate the author's idea)

- The author's mood in the passage (Is the author being humorous? Critical? Bitter? Reflective? How does he or she *feel*?)

- The author's point of view (What's the author's attitude toward the subject? How does he or she make you as a reader feel about the topic?)

- Your own conclusions about the subject (What conclusions can you draw from what you've read?)

- The author's method of making his or her point

Teacher-made tests generally are limited to the first two of these topics, but you always have to be prepared for the teacher who may use all six.

Sentence Completions

Another way test-makers measure your reading comprehension is by asking you to fill in the blanks in sentences from which words have been omitted. This kind of question tests your ability to find the word or words that best fit the logic and style of the rest of the sentence. To do this correctly, you must have a clear understanding of the sentence and its implications. Here is a sample question and explanation from a College Board *PSAT/NMSQT Student Bulletin,* followed by two questions from the same source for you to try on your own (answers are on page 64).

> If we survey the development of dancing as an art in Europe, we recognize two streams of tradition which have sometimes ------- and yet remain essentially -------.
>
> (A) changed . . modern   (B) divided . . separate
>   (C) abated . . primitive   (D) merged . . distinct
>   (E) advanced . . comparable

In this sentence there are two strong clues to the pair of words that must fill the blanks. First, the sentence focuses on the fact that the development of dancing exhibits "two streams of tradition." The missing words must further describe that dual development. The second clue is the construction: "have sometimes . . . and yet remain. . . ." This suggests that the conclusion of the sentence refers to an apparent contradiction. The words that fill the blanks must express this contradiction. Of the five choices, choice (D), *merged . . distinct*, best satisfies both requirements. *Merged* and *distinct* are both appropriate words to apply to "two streams of tradition," and their contradictory meanings make them appropriate words in the construction: "have sometimes . . . and yet remain. . . ." As a final test of correctness, insertion of the words in the sentence yields a meaningful English sentence.

Each sentence below has one or two blanks, each blank indicating that something has been omitted. Beneath the sentence are five lettered words or sets of words. Choose the word or set of words that *best* fits the meaning of the sentence as a whole.

(6) Although its publicity has been -------, the film itself is intelligent, well-acted, handsomely produced, and altogether -------.

   (A) tasteless . . respectable   (B) extensive . . moderate
     (C) sophisticated . . amateur   (D) risqué . . crude
       (E) perfect . . spectacular

(7) Precision of wording is necessary in good writing; by choosing words that exactly convey the desired meaning, one can avoid -------.

   (A) duplicity   (B) incongruity   (C) complexity
   (D) ambiguity   (E) implications

Tests of vocabulary. The ability to do well on a vocabulary test appears to be related to the ability to do well in school subjects. For this reason, vocabulary tests turn up in all sorts of measures of academic ability as well as in tests of language and verbal skills. There are many kinds of vocabulary questions. Here are a few.

Antonyms (Opposites)

A common way to test your vocabulary is through the use of antonyms, or opposites. In each question, a word is given and you're asked to select from five words the one that's most nearly opposite in meaning to the given word. Here are some sample directions, questions, and explanations of the answers adapted from a College Board publication:

> Each question below consists of a word in capital letters, followed by five lettered words or phrases. Choose the word or phrase that is most nearly opposite in meaning to the word in capital letters. Since some of the questions require you to distinguish fine shades of meaning, consider all the choices before deciding which is best.

AGILE: **(A)** humble **(B)** clumsy **(C)** useless **(D)** timid **(E)** ugly

Since *agile* means quick, dexterous, and easy in movement, the best answer is (B), *clumsy*, which means slow, awkward, and ungainly in movement, the most nearly opposite in meaning to *agile*. If you know the meaning of the word *agile*, choices (A), (C), (D), and (E) are obviously incorrect.

SUBJUGATE: **(A)** excuse **(B)** justify **(C)** chastise **(D)** liberate **(E)** oversee

Subjugate means to conquer, force submission, or enslave. Therefore, the correct answer is (D), *liberate*, which means to release from bondage. The other four choices don't convey any meaning opposite to that of *subjugate*.

Now try these (from *About the* SAT, College Board, 1977). The answers are on page 64.

> (8) COMPOSURE: **(A)** analysis **(B)** alertness **(C)** contrast **(D)** agitation **(E)** destruction
>
> (9) SCHISM: **(A)** majority **(B)** union **(C)** uniformity **(D)** conference **(E)** construction

Synonyms

Another way to test your vocabulary is through the use of synonyms, words that have the same or nearly the same meaning. In each question, a word is given and you're asked to select from five words the one that has most nearly the same meaning as the given word.

Try the two questions below. Each test word, in capital letters, is followed by five possible answers. The correct answer is the word that means most nearly the same as the test word. You'll find the answers on page 64.

(10) FREQUENTLY: (A) always (B) often (C) never (D) very (E) soon

(11) SCOLD: (A) upbraid (B) gripe (C) warn (D) twit (E) embarrass

Analogies

Of all the objective test questions, verbal analogies are the most puzzling to inexperienced test-takers. These questions don't look like anything you ever set out to learn. They even look artificial. So why is it that these questions turn up in tests and are thought of so highly by school people?

The answer is that a verbal-analogy question is a condensed and very efficient test of verbal reasoning. It calls upon you to demonstrate your recollection of words and your sensitivity to their meanings. You're given two or three parts of a verbal problem and are asked to supply one or two parts that are missing.

Sometimes it's just the form of the analogy test question that confuses people:

Up : Down : : Out : _____

If you read the colon (:) as shorthand for the phrase "is related to" and the double colon (::) in the middle as shorthand for "as" or "just like" or "in the same way as," you can put these words into a sentence that makes sense. It becomes:

Up is related to down in the same way as out is related to _____.

Since up is the opposite of down, and the opposite of out is in, then the answer has to be *in*. The translated sentence reads:

Up is related to down in the same way as out is related to in.

So when you come upon an analogies question that puzzles you, read the analogy as a question, forgetting about the colons. The sample above reads as follows:

Up is related to down in the same way as out is related to *what*?

This procedure won't tell you what the answer is, but it will help you get the question straightened out so you can understand it.

Once you understand the question, you've got to look for the relationship between the words or elements in the first pair given. In the sample above, the relationship between up and down is that they are opposites; so you try to think of a word that is the opposite of out. But there are many relationships that are not opposites; some analogies, for example, ask you to think of a word that has the same or nearly the same meaning. Here are some relationships commonly found in verbal analogies tests:*

Relationship	*Example*
means the same as (opposite of)	wrath : anger
is a type of or an adjective describing	Merino : sheep
is a part of	spring : watch
usually becomes or comes before	tadpole : frog
is a cause (effect) of	puncture : "blow-out"
usually goes with	bacon : eggs
is used to (done by)	mop : clean
is used by (uses)	hammer : carpenter
is made from or made of	clothing : fabric
is a larger (smaller) version of	lake : pond
is more (less) than	hard : formidable
is a measure of	mile : distance
has the purpose of	perspiration : cooling
is located in (by or around)	Chicago : Illinois

There's no need to try to memorize these things; it's enough if you know generally what kinds of relationships turn up in verbal-analogy questions and then let your mind run free during the test.

You can eliminate some wrong answers in a multiple-choice analogy question by looking at the grammatical structure of the question as you have translated it into English. A properly completed analogy will always have identical pairs of parts of speech, so you can at least determine what part of speech the answer ought to be. If the first, second, and third elements in an analogy are verbs, the missing element is almost certain to be a verb.

walk : run : : speak : (shout or yell)

---

*From *How to Take Tests* by Jason Millman and Walter Pauk. Copyright © 1969, McGraw-Hill Book Company. Used with the permission of McGraw-Hill Book Company.

Or if the first two elements are alike, then the missing one must be of the same part of speech as the third.

loud : noisy : : soft : (quiet)

There is a verbal-analogy question type in which you are asked to choose both the third and fourth elements with only the first and second given. This type often turns up in the College Board's Scholastic Aptitude Test. Here's an example from a *PSAT/NMSQT Student Bulletin:*

> Each question below consists of a related pair of words or phrases, followed by five lettered pairs of words or phrases. Select the lettered pair that *best* expresses a relationship similar to that expressed in the original pair.
>
> EGG : BIRD : : **(A) cell : muscle   (B) acorn : oak**
> **(C) implication : crime   (D) motion : flight**
>   **(E) earth : vegetable**

Here's the explanation of the answer given in the *Bulletin:*

> *Bird* and *egg* are related because a bird develops from an egg; therefore, a similar relationship must exist between the words of the correct answer. The words of choice (B) meet this requirement, since an *oak* develops from an *acorn*. Choice (E) may seem correct if an egg is considered as a place or source of nourishment from which a bird develops, but a *vegetable* develops from the *earth* in only a very general sense; it is clear that the relationship between an *oak* and an *acorn* is more similar to that between a *bird* and an *egg*.

Now try these two questions from the Graduate Record Examinations (taken from a *GRE Information Bulletin*). The answers are on page 64.

(12) COLOR : SPECTRUM : : **(A) tone : scale**
        (B) sound : waves   (C) verse : poem
          (D) dimension : space   (E) cell : organism

(13) GRIEVANCE : REDRESS : : **(A) crime : imprisonment**
        (B) reprisal : restitution   (C) will : settlement
          (D) sorrow : pleasure   (E) loss : compensation

Tests of spelling. For certain kinds of jobs (and for certain kinds of teachers), your skill at spelling is known to be important. You've had many teacher-made tests of spelling—tests in which the teacher dictates one word at a time and you write each word out carefully so that your writing can be read. But here are some types of spelling questions you might not have seen:

Finding Misspelled Words

In 14 and 15 below, you are to look for a misspelled word. If you think all the words are spelled correctly, your answer choice will be (E).

(14) (A) reliance
(B) disturbance
(C) occurrance
(D) ordinance
(E) none misspelled

(15) (A) carefulness
(B) skillfully
(C) wishfull
(D) successful
(E) none misspelled

In the following sentence, there are several underlined words. Look at each one of the underlined words and decide whether one of them is *not* spelled correctly. If you decide that all of them *are* spelled correctly, your answer choice will be (E).

(16) <u>Featured</u> in the <u>exhibition</u> were <u>sculptures</u> by Selma
     A   B   C
Burke and <u>portraites</u> by Archibald Motley. <u>No error</u>
       D   E

There are many variations on the theme of getting you to recognize a misspelled word when you see one in print. There is evidence that if you are good at the kind of proofreading required in question 16 above, you are also good at spelling in your own writing.

Tests of writing. Essay tests are not the only method of measuring your writing skill. Test-makers have devised other ways of measuring different aspects of writing ability. Here are some sample English composition questions from CLEP *General and Subject Examinations*, 1979-80. The answers are on page 64.

Directions: For each of these questions, you are to choose the version of the underlined sentence or part of the sentence that not only has the same or nearly the same meaning as the original but follows the requirements of standard written English. That is, in selecting the version that matches the underlined part in meaning, pay attention to grammar, choice of words, sentence structure, and punctuation. The answer you select should, when inserted in the original sentence, produce an effective sentence—clear and exact, without awkwardness or ambiguity.

Example:

Sometimes we wonder when we should take action, not what action to take.

   (A) Sometimes the question is when to take action
   (B) Sometimes the question is in the nature of when action is taken
   (C) The question sometimes relates to the time to take action
   (D) The question sometimes is of when action is taken
   (E) Sometimes the question is the time of taking action

SAMPLE QUESTIONS

(17) Because of his efforts to secure civil rights, Dr. King was put in the city jail.

   (A) arrested and they took him to
   (B) arrested, being taken to
   (C) arrested, and he had been taken to
   (D) arrested and taken to
   (E) arrested; they had taken him to

(18) His failure to realize that time was running out caused Clark not to shoot before the buzzer.

   (A) His failure to realize that time was running out was the cause why Clark did not shoot before the buzzer.
   (B) Not realizing that time was running out, Clark failed to shoot before the buzzer.
   (C) He failed to realize that time was running out, which was why Clark did not shoot before the buzzer.
   (D) Clark did not realize time was running out, causing the failure to shoot before the buzzer.
   (E) Clark did not shoot before the buzzer insofar as he failed to realize time was running out.

(19) **The more Victoria thought about what she had done,
the greater her sorrow.**

    (A) increasingly she felt sadly
    (B) she felt increasingly sadder
    (C) the more sadly she felt
    (D) the more she felt sadly
    (E) the sadder she felt

Tests of listening ability. These are not tests of your ability to hear what is spoken to you but to understand the meaning of spoken language. You listen to an essay or a story or an article that your examiner reads to you or that's played on a recording, and then you answer questions about it on a printed page or an answer sheet.

The listening test most widely used is different from reading tests in a way that makes it harder: The passage and the questions are both read to you. So what you see in your test booklet when you open it is simply a series of answer choices for questions that are not there. This means that you can't skim the questions before you listen to the passage the way you might do with a reading test. So there's nothing to do but shut off all other signals and listen.

Here is an example of what a teacher or test administrator might read to you at a listening test (adapted from *Sequential Tests of Educational Progress*—original series):

> Maoris are people who live on the main islands of New Zealand. Many hundreds of years ago the Maoris lived on the Society Islands. They had no written language. But for hundreds of years, the elders of the tribes have passed on the history of the Maoris in song and story. Some songs and stories describe the travels of Kupe (Koop) and other seamen who visited New Zealand.
>
> In the year 1350, the Maoris decided to leave the Society Islands, their original home. The islands were becoming too crowded and food was scarce. The Maoris planned to visit the southern land of their songs and stories. They built a fleet of canoes, loaded them with food, water, and animals, and set out for the new land.
>
> Their trip was long and difficult. Storms lashed them about in the angry seas and their food and water ran low. The Maoris had no compasses or other instruments to guide them across the uncharted Pacific. They used only the position of the sun and stars to guide them to the new land. After many weeks of hardships, they arrived in New Zealand.
>
> When they marked the 600th anniversary of their arrival, it was found that there were over 100,000 Maoris living in New Zealand.

After reading the passage aloud, the examiner would ask questions, and you would select answers from the ones given in your test booklet.

(20) Most people would consider the voyage of the Maoris

(A) courageous (B) common
  (C) unnecessary (D) unimportant

(21) It seems probable that the Maori population

(E) has never been counted
(F) has been slowly dying out in New Zealand
(G) has increased since the Maoris came to New Zealand
(H) has remained about the same since 1350

(22) In order for the Maoris to reach their new home, which of the following bodies of water did they cross?

(A) The Atlantic Ocean (B) The Indian Ocean
  (C) The North Sea (D) None of these

(23) The Maoris must have used only the sun and the stars to guide them because

(E) they were on the sea only a few days
(F) they had no compasses
(G) they wrote about it in a book
(H) they had been to New Zealand many times before

(24) From what the speaker has said, the Maoris were NOT

(A) storytellers (B) singers
  (C) writers (D) navigators

(25) This selection is mainly a description of

(E) the resettlement of the Maoris
(F) Kupe and his seamen
(G) the Maori language
(H) the uncharted ocean

(26) Which of the following statements is unrelated to the rest of the selection?

(A) The Society Islands were overcrowded.
(B) The Maoris had songs and stories.
(C) The Maoris arrived safely in New Zealand.
(D) The Society Islands are not heavily populated today.

Answer Key (Verbal)

(1) C	(8) D	(15) C	(21) G
(2) F	(9) B	(16) D	(22) D
(3) A	(10) B	(17) D	(23) F
(4) E	(11) A	(18) B	(24) C
(5) D	(12) A	(19) E	(25) E
(6) A	(13) E	(20) A	(26) D
(7) D	(14) C		

Mathematical Skills

Mathematics tests generally involve more paper and pencil work than other types of multiple-choice tests. For example, consider the following problem from *Taking the* SAT, College Board, 1978:

If $2x + 2x + 2x = 12$, then $2x - 1 =$

(A) 2   (B) 3   (C) 4   (D) 5   (E) 6

To solve this problem, it's helpful to do a little scratchwork. Since $2x + 2x + 2x = 6x$, a person's scratchwork could appear as follows:

$$6x = 12$$
$$x = 2$$
$$2x - 1 = 3$$

So the correct answer choice is (B). Although some of these steps could be done in your head, it's sometimes safer to write them down. This way you are less likely to make a mistake. Also, make sure you pay attention to what the problem asks for. In this case, $x = 2$, but you are asked to find $2x - 1$.

Before you take any test, make sure you understand the directions. These may be available before you take the test. On some multiple-choice tests, you are penalized for guessing. If there's a penalty for guessing, it is usually to your advantage to guess *if* you can eliminate *one or more* of the choices as wrong. For example, if the answer choices are (A) -3, (B) 1, (C) 2, (D) 5, (E) 7, and the only thing you are sure about is that the answer is *not* negative, you should guess among choices (B) to (E). If there is no penalty for guessing, you should answer *every* question.

There are several types of questions used on mathematics tests. Examples of some of them are discussed below.

Type 1. Arithmetic questions are often presented in a form convenient for carrying out calculations without having to copy the problem. But sometimes you must copy the problem. Examples of each type are shown below. (The second problem comes from the College Board's brochure, *Descriptive Tests of Language and Mathematics Skills*, 1979.)

(1) $\begin{array}{r} 26 \\ \times\ 18 \\ \hline \end{array}$

(A) 234
(B) 428
(C) 462
(D) 468

(2) $15.4 \div 44 =$

(A) 0.28
(B) 0.35
(C) 2.8
(D) 3.5

In question 1, there's space to work the problem without having to copy it somewhere else. In question 2, the best thing to do is copy the question in the form $44\overline{)15.4}$ to carry out the division. Notice that the problem says 15.4 divided by 44, *not* 44 divided by 15.4. If you like, work the problems as you go. The answers are on page 68.

Type 2. For some questions, you have to consider each choice before you can decide which *one* is correct. For this type of question, there's no way to answer the question without considering the choices. Here's an example:

(3) **If x is an even number and y is an odd number, which of the following is an even number?**

(A) $x + y$ (B) $2x + y$ (C) $x + 2y$ (D) $3(x + y)$

In solving problems of this type, it's helpful to remember that the sum of an even number and an odd number is odd, while the sum of two even numbers is even. Again, make sure that you know exactly what you're looking for before you start looking at the choices.

Type 3. Many tests have word problems that require you to apply basic arithmetic to practical situations. The following example is also from the College Board's brochure, *Descriptive Tests of Language and Mathematics Skills*, 1979:

(4) **Karen bought a cola and 2 hamburgers for $2.03. If the cola was $0.25, how much did each hamburger cost?**

(A) $0.89 (B) $0.95 (C) $0.99 (D) $1.78

Notice that this question asks how much did *each* hamburger cost. Look for key words in problems that tell you what to do. You may find it helpful to underline key words or phrases.

Type 4. Many questions in mathematics involve "If . . ., then . . ." logic. The "if" statement is basically what you are *given* to work with, while the "then" statement is what you are *asked to find.* Some examples of this type are included among the types already discussed. The following algebra problem from *Taking the* SAT, 1978, is another example:

(5) If 2a + b = 5, then what is the value of 4a + 2b?

(A) $\frac{5}{4}$ (B) $\frac{5}{2}$ (C) 10 (D) 20

 (E) It cannot be determined from the information given.

For this question, you have to decide how the "if" information relates to the "then" information. By observing that 4a + 2b = 2(2a + b), and using the *given* information 2a + b = 5, it's fairly easy to conclude that 4a + 2b = 10. Notice that the following question is similar to the question above, but has a different answer:

(6) If 2a + b = 5, then what is the value of 2a + 2b?

(A) $\frac{5}{2}$ (B) $\frac{11}{2}$ (C) 10 (D) 25

 (E) It cannot be determined from the information given.

In this case it's *not* possible to use the "if" information to answer the question.

Type 5. Some types of problems are a whole lot easier to solve if you draw a sketch. Consider the following seemingly complicated problem from *Taking the* SAT, 1978:

(7) **The town of Mason is located on Eagle Lake. The town of Canton is west of Mason. Sinclair is east of Canton, but west of Mason. Dexter is east of Richmond, but west of Sinclair and Canton. Assuming all these towns are in the United States, which town is farthest west?**

 (A) Mason (B) Dexter (C) Canton
 (D) Sinclair (E) Richmond

For this kind of problem, drawing a sketch will probably help. In this case, a line can be used to locate the relative position of each town. Start with the statement "The town of Canton is west of Mason" and, using abbreviations, draw the following:

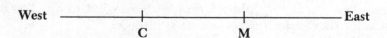

From the remaining information, place the other towns in their correct order:

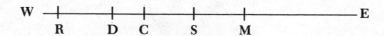

The final sketch shows the town farthest west. Notice how much easier this problem becomes when you sketch it.

Type 6. Some questions, like the one below from *Taking the* SAT, 1978, require you to express the final answer in a special way.

(8) **If the average of v and w is p and the average of x, y, and z is q, what is the average of v, w, x, y, and z in terms of p and q?**

(A) $p + q$ (B) $\dfrac{p + q}{2}$ (C) $2p + 3q$

(D) $\dfrac{2p + 3q}{5}$ (E) $\dfrac{3p + 2q}{5}$

Normally, to find the average of v, w, x, y, and z, you would compute $\dfrac{v + w + x + y + z}{5}$. However, the problem asks you to express the average in terms of p and q. From the fact that the average of v and w is p, you can write $\dfrac{v + w}{2} = p$. This makes $v + w = 2p$. Similarly, $x + y + z = 3q$. Using these facts, the required average $\dfrac{(v + w) + (x + y + z)}{5}$ becomes $\dfrac{2p + 3q}{5}$. Note that choice (B) is the average of p and q and, although tempting, is *not* what you are asked to find. Again, be a careful reader and do scratchwork when it seems helpful.

Type 7. The following geometry question from *About the* SAT is fairly hard to solve, but you can make some progress toward the solution by eliminating clearly impossible answers. Read the question and see how many choices you can rule out before looking at the discussion that follows the question.

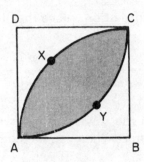

(9) In square ABCD above, if AB = 4 and AXC and AYC are arcs of circles with centers B and D, respectively, what is the area of the shaded region?

(A) $16 - 8\pi$ (B) $4\pi - 8$ (C) $8\pi - 16$
(D) $4 + 4\pi$ (E) $16\pi - 4$

In some questions, even if you're not sure of the solution you may find it worthwhile to guess after you've eliminated some of the answer choices as obviously wrong by common sense or a little arithmetic approximation. For example, in the problem above, side AB of the square has length 4, and therefore the area of the square is 16. You might then compare the answer choices with the area of the square. Choice (A) can be eliminated by inspection if you remember that π is a number greater than 3 and that therefore $16 - 8\pi$ is a negative number—a logically impossible answer. Both (D) and (E) are choices greater than 16—certainly incorrect answers because the shaded area would then be greater than the area of the square. After eliminating these three choices, you are left with (B) and (C), the only possible answers. The chances are 50-50 that you'll get the question right by guessing one of these.

It's important to understand that this kind of guessing can be worthwhile even if the test has a scoring penalty for guessing, because some of the choices can be eliminated as *definitely* wrong. When there's no scoring penalty on a multiple-choice test, you should always guess.

Answer Key (Mathematics)

(1) D	(4) A	(6) E	(8) D
(2) B	(5) C	(7) E	(9) C
(3) C			

The Sciences

Most tests in science measure your ability to apply your knowledge in the solution of problems. That's why science tests usually have drawings, graphs, charts, and so forth. The important thing for a test like this is to make sure you understand the problem before you start to look for its solution. Sometimes, students make quick assumptions about a problem and ignore important information in the question itself. So double-check the problem before you jump for an answer.

Educators divide the sciences into two main groups: physical sciences and biological sciences. Physical sciences include astronomy, physics, chemistry, and the various cousins of these subjects. Biological sciences include biology, agronomy, health sciences—those that pertain to living things. Here are some sample questions in the physical sciences. Answers are on page 72.

The Physics of Time (adapted from STEP Science, original series)

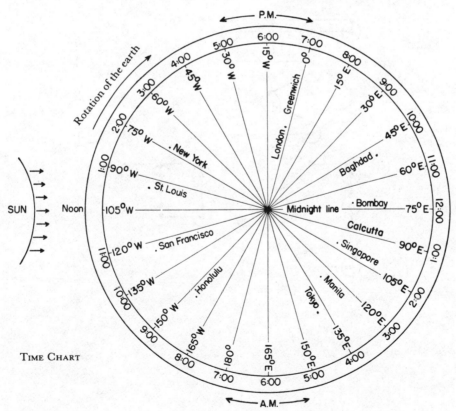

TIME CHART

(1) One could determine from the time chart that when it is noon, April 11, in Honolulu, the date and time in Baghdad is

(E) April 11, 1:00 a.m.
(F) April 11, 11:00 a.m.
(G) April 12, 1:00 a.m.
(H) April 12, noon

Electricity (adapted from STEP Science, original series)

(2) A circuit is to have a 50-volt source and a current of 0.25 ampere. According to Ohm's law, the resistance of the circuit should be

(E) 0.005 ohm   (F) 12.5 ohms
  (G) 20 ohms   (H) 200 ohms

(3) In a certain circuit, you need 6 volts and very little current. You decide to use 1½-volt dry cells. Of the following, the correct arrangement is

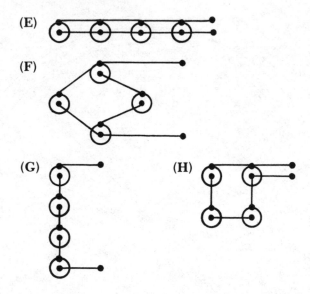

Here are some sample questions in the biological sciences. Answers are on page 72.

Aspects of Genetics
(from the College Board's *About the Achievement Tests*)

(4) An animal breeder crossed a black and a white guinea pig and a litter of three black offspring resulted. The breeder concluded that the black parent could not have been heterozygous (hybrid) for coat color because he thought that any cross between a black heterozygous guinea pig and a white guinea pig would yield a ratio of one black to one white offspring. His conclusion was unsound because he failed to realize that

(A) the black parent may have been a male
(B) mutations in coat color frequently occur
(C) coat color in guinea pigs is not inherited
(D) black coat color is dominant over white in guinea pigs
(E) genetic ratios are reliable only for large numbers of offspring

Cell Characteristics
(from the College Board's *About the Achievement Tests*)

A GENERALIZED ANIMAL CELL

(5) Aerobic respiration occurs in
    (A) 1   (B) 2   (C) 5   (D) 6   (E) 7

(6) The genetic code is carried in
    (A) 1   (B) 2   (C) 4   (D) 5   (E) 7

General Biology (7, 8, and 10 from the College Board's brochure, CLEP *General and Subject Examinations*; 9 from the College Board's *Advanced Placement Course Description—Biology*, May 1982)

(7) In which of the following ways do social insects benefit most from having several types or castes within the species?

(A) Each colony is able to include a large number of individuals.
(B) The secretions or odors produced by the protective caste are an effective defense.
(C) The division of the species into castes insures the survival of the fittest.
(D) Large numbers of the worker caste can migrate to start new colonies.
(E) The specialized structure of each caste permits greater division of labor.

(8) Which cell structures are primarily involved in the oxidation processes?

(A) Nucleoli   (B) Mitochondria   (C) Ribosomes
(D) Nuclei   (E) Centrosomes

(9) A metabolic study of a natural community revealed that the energy released via respiration exceeded the energy captured in photosynthesis. Which of the following conditions prevailed?

(A) Community biomass was decreasing.
(B) Community biomass was increasing.
(C) The first law of thermodynamics was not operating.
(D) The second law of thermodynamics was not operating.
(E) This is a climax community.

(10) Which of the following did Mendel infer from his data?

(A) Linkage   (B) Crossing over between genes
(C) Independent assortment of genes
(D) Mutation   (E) Nondisjunction of gene pairs

Answer Key (The Sciences)

(1) G	(4) E	(7) E	(9) A
(2) H	(5) B	(8) B	(10) C
(3) G	(6) E		

The Social Sciences

In recent years, what used to be called "social studies" (history, geography, economics, sociology, and government) has expanded to include dozens of special fields, but below the level of advanced college courses much instruction in the social sciences is concentrated in the five subfields mentioned above.

As you well know, there are many different courses in history: American history, modern world history, European history, African history, and so on. Tests in history have a large number of questions that ask you to remember names, dates, incidents, and results and that ask you to interpret the meaning of charts and graphs and cartoons. They ask questions about why things happened the way they did, what the consequences of certain historical events have been, and what implications those events might have for the future.

Geography is a field of social science that's now included in such courses as "world problems" or "modern civilization." Geography tests often feature maps and graphs and photographs and questions about the facts of places and products and climate. Also, there are still a lot of the old "What is the capital of Peru?" types. Following are some sample questions. The answers are on page 77.

Cartoon Interpretation (from the College Board's brochure, *CLEP General and Subject Examinations*)

(1) **The cartoon above refers to the**

    (A) Napoleonic Wars   (B) Crimean War
    (C) Boer War   (D) Russo-Japanese War
    (E) First World War

Some questions, like the one below adapted from the College Board publication *About the Achievement Tests*, require knowledge of facts, terms, and concepts. They test your ability to recall basic information about significant historical developments.

>   (2) **The predominant religion in colonial New England was**
>
>   (A) **Anglican**   (B) **Lutheran**   (C) **Quaker**
>   (D) **Congregational**   (E) **Baptist**
>
>   (3) **All of the following conditions experienced by blacks in the pre-Civil-War North were also encountered by black residents of northern cities in the 1960's EXCEPT**
>
>   (A) **substandard housing**
>   (B) **legal disfranchisement**
>   (C) **inferior public education**
>   (D) **discrimination in employment**
>   (E) **hostility from white ethnic minorities**

Other questions, like the one below adapted from the same College Board publication, require the ability to select or apply hypotheses, concepts, principles, or generalizations to given data. These questions may begin with a statement of facts and ask you to generalize from them, or they may begin with a concept and ask you to apply it to particular problems or situations.

>   (4) **From 1900 to 1960, hours worked have been steadily reduced, while both money wages and real wages have continued to rise. What factor is primarily responsible for this trend?**
>
>   (A) **A reduction in profit margins**
>   (B) **Minimum wage laws**
>   (C) **Restriction of the labor supply**
>   (D) **Increased output per man-hour**
>   (E) **Right-to-work legislation**

The following is a question requiring map interpretation (from *Multiple-Choice Questions: A Close Look*, Educational Testing Service, 1963). You are asked to make inferences from the data that are given you on the map of the imaginary country, Serendip. *The answers in most instances must be probabilities rather than certainties.* The relative size of towns and cities is not shown. To assist you in the location of the places mentioned in the questions, the map is divided into squares lettered vertically from A to E and numbered horizontally from 1 to 5.

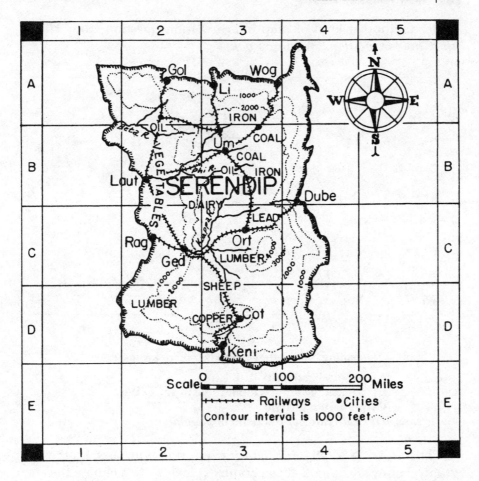

(5) Which of the following cities would be the best location for a steel mill?

(A) Li   (3A)
(B) Um   (3B)
(C) Cot   (3D)
(D) Dube   (4B)

Here's another kind of map interpretation question from *Multiple-Choice Questions: A Close Look.*

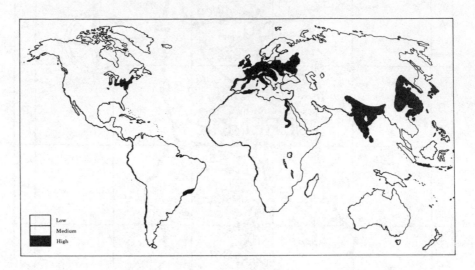

(6) **The shading on the above map is used to indicate**

    (A) **population density**
    (B) **percentage of total labor force in agriculture**
    (C) **per capita income**
    (D) **death rate per thousand of population**

The following graph interpretation questions are based on the two graphs below. First look at the graphs quickly. Then choose the correct answer to each question. You may look back at the graphs as often as you need to in answering the questions.

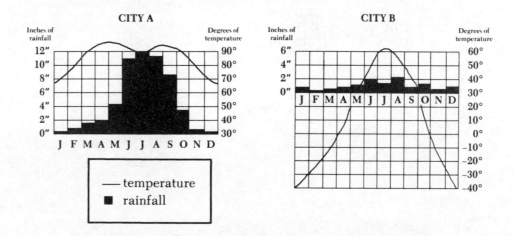

(7) What is the average temperature of city A in February?

(A) Between 8° and 10°
(B) Between –30° and –40°
(C) Between 60° and 70°
(D) About 80°
(E) The graph does not show this.

(8) What conclusion *cannot* be drawn about the climate of these two cities?

(A) Types of clothing needed in city A would be different from those needed in city B.
(B) The coldest months in city A are also the coldest months in city B.
(C) The annual temperature range is greater in city B than in city A.
(D) The three months of greatest rainfall in city B are also the three months of greatest rainfall in city A.
(E) City B is in the Northern Hemisphere and city A is in the Southern Hemisphere.

Answer Key (The Social Sciences)

(1) E	(3) B	(5) B	(7) D
(2) D	(4) D	(6) A	(8) E

Vocational Aptitude Tests

The aptitudes that are considered in training and qualifying for jobs are learned skills. Some people have more of a certain aptitude than others, but whatever it is, they learned it; it's an acquired skill that grows out of how the individual acts upon and responds to what's going on in his or her world. People with musical aptitude, for example, often come from musical backgrounds. Most major league baseball players grew up in environments that surrounded them with competitive sports. So any test of your aptitude for something measures a mix of your skills in that particular thing, your experience in doing it, your interest in it, and the richness of your background in it.

There are many different kinds of tests in the general category of vocational aptitude tests. With a name like that, you'd expect that these tests would measure your skills and knowledge related to getting a job you want or finding work that you'd like to do. Most of the vocational aptitude tests are intended to do just that, but many of them look like the tests you take in school. Actually, there are some tests that are used both for finding out about your skill in school subjects and your probable success on a job. For example, tests of reading comprehension turn up frequently both in school testing and in occupational testing because skill in reading is important not only in school but in many jobs. Vocational aptitude tests, however, usually include some additional kinds of questions that are not in the regular school achievement tests—questions to measure such things as clerical speed and accuracy (your speed and skill in seeing and marking letter and number symbols) or mechanical reasoning (your ability to understand and apply simple physical laws and forces).

All of the suggestions given in Chapters 2, 3, and 4—finding out about the test ahead of time, preparing yourself as well as you can, and things to remember while taking the test—apply just as much to vocational aptitude tests as they do to tests given for school purposes.

Vocational tests for guidance. These are the tests and test batteries used by school and college counselors to help students find out some of the things they do best and in this way guide them into thinking in practical ways about making their choices of occupational fields. The Differential Aptitude Test, which is given most often to students in the ninth grade who are planning their high school courses, is one of the most widely used tests of this kind. This test and the several others in this category have one section devoted to testing your skill with words and another devoted to numbers. In addition, these tests usually measure:

- *Abstract reasoning*—measuring your power to understand and apply ideas expressed in diagrams rather than words or pictures

- *Clerical speed and accuracy*—measuring your skill and speed in seeing and marking letters and numbers

- *Mechanical reasoning*—getting at your ability to understand and apply simple physical laws and forces by using pictures of pulleys and levers

- *Space relations*—testing your ability to visualize solids and structural shapes (looking first at a picture of a shape and then in your mind turning it over and around to visualize what it looks like in its new position)

Vocational tests for admission to specialized kinds of training. Schools that give special training for certain vocations use these tests. A good secretarial school, for example, will give its applicants a battery of tests that includes measures of reading speed and accuracy, sharpness of eyesight, clarity of speech and written expression (possibly a short essay test), speed in sorting or matching file cards, and skills in typing and shorthand. A college of engineering will test applicants in advanced mathematics, mechanical drawing, space relations, and perhaps principles of mechanics. For the most part, these tests explore your general background and don't go into your specific job skills.

Tests for licensing and certification. Nearly all of these contain some form of the tests you've been taking all through school (How well can you read? How well can you speak? How well can you write? How well can you work with numbers?) with some extra tasks that require you to demonstrate your job skill.

Here are some questions that illustrate the kinds of problems you might find on a certification test for automobile mechanics. These sample questions are taken from the 1980 National Institute for Automotive Service Excellence Bulletin of Information. The answers are on page 82.

(1) The front wheel bearings of a car are to be adjusted.

Mechanic A says that a torque wrench can be used to set the initial preload.

Mechanic B says that a dial indicator can be used to set the initial preload.

Who is right?

(A) A only   (B) B only
    (C) Both A and B   (D) Neither A nor B

(2) A car with power steering is running at fast idle. A buzzing noise is heard when the wheels are straight ahead. The noise stops as the wheels are turned. Which of these could be the cause?

(A) A blocked high pressure line
(B) A sticking pressure control valve
(C) A misadjusted steering gear
(D) A loose pump belt

(3) **The front end of a car with disc/drum brakes dips too much when the brakes are lightly applied. What is the most likely cause?**

(A) Loose front wheel bearings
(B) Air in the front brake lines
(C) Binding caliper piston seals
(D) Bad metering (hold off) valve

A person who wants to be licensed as a manicurist might find questions like the following on a state licensing test (from the *Information Booklet for Applicants Taking the Qualifying Examinations for Licensure in the Cosmetology Field*, State Board of Cosmetology, Commonwealth of Pennsylvania):

(4) **Which of the diagrams below show(s) a correct way to file a fingernail?**

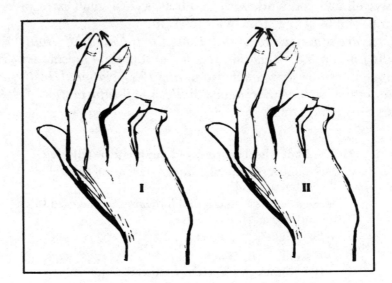

(A) I only   (B) II only
(C) Both I and II   (D) Neither I nor II

(5) **Which of the following statements about manicuring is (are) true?**

I. A sharp pointed instrument is used to clean under the nails.
II. A styptic pencil is used to stop bleeding for a small cut.

(A) I only   (B) II only
(C) Both I and II   (D) Neither I nor II

(6) Nail polish is about to be applied over an artificial nail-building solution. The condition of the solution must be which of the following?

(A) Semidry and smooth   **(B)** Wet and smooth
   (C) Semidry and rough   **(D)** Dry and smooth

Here are some types of questions people who want to be fire fighters have to answer (from the *Pre-Examination Booklet for the Philadelphia Fire Department Fire Fighter Examination*):

Observation of Details

The picture below and the sample questions test your ability to be a careful observer and accurately notice details. You do NOT need to memorize the sample picture. In the test, you will be able to look at the pictures in order to answer the questions.

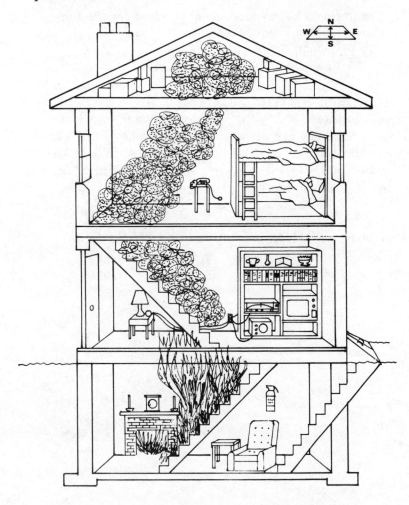

Answer the following questions based on the picture of the house.

(7) Of the following, the most likely fire hazard in the house is the

    (A) television set   (B) electrical outlet
      (C) radio   (D) record player

(8) How many ways can fire fighters enter the house?

    (A) One   (B) Two   (C) Three   (D) Four

(9) The probable cause of the fire was

    (A) sparks from the fireplace
    (B) the overloaded electrical outlet
    (C) the combustion of flammable materials in the attic
    (D) smoking in bed

(10) What would be the most direct entrance for the fire fighters to take to save the children?

    (A) East window   (B) West window
      (C) Front door   (D) Basement door

There are licensing and certification tests in almost every field you can think of, but there's space here to show only a few. All have one thing in common: They are designed to measure how much knowledge or skill you have in a certain field or fields. What skills are essential to succeed in the kind of work you want to do? Make a list of them; they'll be in any test you take to get a job or a license.

Answer Key (Tests for Licensing and Certification)

(1) A	(4) B	(7) B	(9) A
(2) B	(5) D	(8) D	(10) A
(3) D	(6) D		

Chapter 7

AFTER THE TEST

- Reviewing
- Understanding your score

Chapter 7

AFTER THE TEST

After you've taken a big test that your teacher prepared, you may think that the thing to do is to celebrate and put the whole thing out of your head. You may be right about the celebrating, but don't put the whole thing out of your head. Why not learn from this one to make the next one easier?

There are some things you really ought to do soon after you take a big test, things that are not hard and that sometimes can be fun.

Reviewing the Test

Review with others who took the test. Talking to others about the test after it's over can be very profitable. If you do this right after the test, the group will be able to remember a big percentage of the questions. Compare the answers you remember giving and try to figure out what the correct answers probably were. In this kind of discussion, you often get the kind of feedback that helps you learn even more than you learn by studying books.

Review by yourself. Not all after-the-test review must be done with others; some of it you should do by yourself. The thing to do is make notes to yourself about what parts of your preparation were successful and what parts were not. What particular topics or problems gave you the most trouble? What kinds of things did you breeze through? What test-taking techniques did you try for the first time and like? Don't make a career of this task; half an hour is enough. But do it soon after the test.

Review with your teachers. You seldom see your teachers immediately after a test, of course, but try to get them to hold a discussion of the test as soon after the event as is convenient for them. If the teacher wants to make the best use of time, he or she will arrange to talk with a whole group rather than just with you alone.

Ask for copies of the test to refer to during the discussion. Then ask the teacher to give you not only the specific answers to all questions but also the reasons why one answer is better than another to a hard question. You can accomplish a lot in a teacher-led discussion of this kind.

Interpreting Your Scores

Different test scores mean different things. If all test scores had generally the same meaning, this book would be a few pages shorter. But there are at least half a dozen different types of test scores that you are likely to encounter and, therefore, should know about.

The three types of test scores you will encounter most often are described below.

- *Norm-based scores* show how well you performed on the test in comparison with other people of the same age or grade or class who have taken the same test in the past. As a group, these normative scores show where your performance put you in competition with others. Some normative scores are expressed as *standard scores*. Others are reported as percentile ranks, which tell you what percent of a group of test-takers earned scores lower than yours. If you have a percentile rank of 60, let's say, that means you scored higher than 60 percent of those who took the same test. A *stanine* score, widely used in some parts of the country, is based on a system that divides the whole range of scores into nine equal segments. Your *stanine* score, therefore, can be any number from 1 (the lowest) to 9 (the highest).

- *Performance-based scores* show how well you performed on the test itself. They tell you whether you were able to handle very little of the test, most of it, all of it, or none of it. These scores have different names ("criterion-related" or "criterion-referenced" scores are some others), but they all tell you the same thing: Instead of comparing you with other people or with your own expectations, they show how well you did on the test itself. The score you get on the written test for a driver's license is an example of a performance-based score. So is the score you get on the Practice Test in the back of this book. Scores on these tests don't tell you how your performance compares with others who took these tests. They simply tell you how much you remembered about the driver's manual and about this book when you took the tests.

- *Profile-type scores* show comparisons of your performance on one kind of test with your performance on other kinds. Such scores often are expressed in graphs or profiles, letting you see quickly how well you did in one subject compared with how you did in others. For example, these scores may indicate that you do better on tests having to do with history and literature than on those having to do with math and science. Or your test performance may have been stronger in space perception and mechanical understanding than it was in clerical skills or speed of reading.

Interpreting scores on teacher-made tests. The meaning of your score on teacher-made tests depends upon what your teacher uses as a standard. He or she may decide that 70 percent is passing, 71-80 is a C, 81-90 is a B and 91-100 is an A or some other arrangement of numbers and letters.

Or your teacher may be interested in using your score to compare your performance on a test with others in the class. The most common way of doing this is to give your score a rank in the class. The teacher simply lines up all the scores in the class from high to low and assigns your score a number which indicates where you rank in the class group, such as eighteenth in a class of 34 or third in a class of 27. With this kind of score, how many correct answers you got is less important than how well you did compared with the rest of the people in the class. If you answered only half the questions correctly but got more of them right than most of the class, you'll earn a high score. Some teachers use both arbitrary scores and comparative scores, depending on the type of test and the circumstance.

Percentile ranks, which were explained on page 86, give the teacher a way of making even more useful comparisons. They enable the teacher to see if you're making progress or slowing down during the year in comparison with others in your class. If your test scores were usually better than 50 percent of the scores in your group at the beginning of the year (if you had a percentile rank of 50 each time) and consistently better than 75 percent of your group at the end of the year (a percentile rank of 75), you've obviously gained on somebody and made progress.

Scores on systemwide and statewide tests. In some school systems, the central office that manages the testing will send you a detailed report of your test performance and will train teachers or counselors to help you understand it. If you have trouble understanding it, ask your teacher (or counselor) for help. The result of your performance on a school-system test will probably be expressed as a percentile rank. If the people in the testing office in your school system use some other score-reporting method, they'll have booklets telling you all about it and how to interpret scores. This will be true whether the tests were given by the school system, the county, or the state.

National testing programs by outside agencies. Nearly always, national testing programs like the College Board and the American College Testing Program make a special effort to report your scores to you in detail. These programs score the tests and send you your scores along with booklets telling you how to interpret them. They'll tell you how your test performance compares with those of thousands of other students with the same background as yours, how it compares with other students seeking admission to college, letting you see exactly how well you're doing in competition with people who want a particular kind of job or a scholarship or admission to graduate school. These programs send your dean or counselor still more information about your test scores. So if you think you could use some help in figuring out what the score reports from these programs mean, ask your counselor; he or she is well prepared to help.

One Last Word

After you've read this book and tried out its techniques on a test, pass it along to a friend. Pass along your know-how, too. Telling somebody how to cope with tests doesn't take away one bit of your skill at test-taking, and it helps you tremendously. It's been known for thousands of years that the best way to learn something is to try to teach it to somebody else. Why not try it with *How to Take a Test?* You'll be glad you did.

REVIEWING WHAT YOU'VE LEARNED

- 100 Ways to improve your test-taking ability
- Test Talk
- Practice test

100 WAYS TO IMPROVE
YOUR TEST-TAKING ABILITY

To Stay on Top of Things...

1. Take your classes and your homework assignments seriously from the very first day of class.

2. Read, read, read. Read newspapers, magazines, fiction, non-fiction, hardbacks, paperbacks.

3. Get some friends together to form a study group such as the one in the TV show, "The Paper Chase."

4. Study regularly. Study often. Review periodically.

5. When you study, focus on (1) facts, (2) comparisons, and (3) relationships.

6. Prepare for tests by taking good lecture notes.

7. Outline a study plan in which you decide what material you will cover, how much time you will spend, and how you will use the time.

8. Don't rely solely on class notes or your own intuition to decide what to study for a test. Find out what is likely to be asked.

9. If possible, find out about specific features of the test including its format.

10. Learn to read and translate tables and charts, using the key or legend that is provided for interpreting the data.

11. Learn to read graphs of all kinds—circle, bar, square, picture, and line—since each presents data in a different way and for a somewhat different purpose.

12. Use any practice materials that are available from the test publisher or from the teacher.

13. Practice problem solving to get used to spacing.

14. Learn as many analogy relationships as possible by studying a list of the main relationships used by writers of test questions.

15. In preparation for a true-false test, commit to memory facts such as names, dates, places, rules, and principles and think about the relationships between facts.

16. Choose a cramming method that is appropriate for the amount of preparation time you have. Prepared cramming for a major test takes at least a week. Intense cramming takes about three days.

17. Review your notes as often as possible before taking the test.

18. Remember that accurate and appropriate use of the technical language of a subject is an indication of your understanding of the subject.

19. Practice as much as possible answering test questions that are out of the ordinary—analogies, for example.

20. Become familiar with standardized test directions and formats ahead of time: multiple-choice, verbal analogy, sentence completion, antonym, reading passage, quantitative comparison.

When it's Time for the Test...

21. Get a good night's sleep.

22. Eat wisely.

23. Wear clothing that is comfortable and appropriate for the occasion and the weather.

24. Wear a watch; be aware of time but not overly conscious of it.

25. Take several sharpened pencils and a good separate eraser.

26. Be punctual.

When You Arrive in the Test Room...

27. If possible, select a seat away from friends who might be distracting to you.

28. If tablet-arm chairs are used and if you are left-handed, ask for a left-handed chair or an arrangement that will be comfortable for you.

29. Don't let anxiety overwhelm you.

30. Be physically relaxed, mentally alert, and feel confident that you will do well.

31. Remember that a test taker who relies *only* on luck will usually earn low scores.

32. Believe in yourself.

33. Listen carefully to directions that are read to you. Test instructions are very important, so it is necessary to thoroughly understand what you are to do.

34. Ask questions immediately if you do not understand the directions.

35. Read directions carefully.

36. Do the practice questions.

37. Plan your time. Begin each test or separately timed section of a test by checking its length and estimating how much time is available for each question.

While You're Taking the Test...

38. Don't rush yourself. Work within your time schedule.

39. Do not make the question more difficult than it acutally is. Answer the question as it is being asked.

40. Read critically; do not read anything into the test question that is not intended.

41. Read the questions carefully; don't jump to conclusions.

42. In a multiple-choice test, always read every answer choice.

43. Work quickly. Don't spend too much time on any one question.

44. On the first pass through a test, answer all the questions that are easy for you; then go back to the hard ones if time permits.

45. Break up long questions or difficult math problems into manageable parts.

46. Don't skip around on reading comprehension passages since they generally do proceed from easy to difficult within the sections of the test.

47. If it is permitted, underline or circle names, numbers, places, and definitions in a reading passage.

48. Make sure that any numbered space you use for an answer has the same number as the question you are answering.

49. Take the time to change an answer if you have good reason for doing so.

50. If you change an answer, erase your previous answer completely. Leave no stray marks on your paper.

51. Check to be sure answers are recorded exactly as the instructions stipulated.

52. If time permits, check your answers.

53. Work out all calculations as a check on the accuracy of your answer choice.

54. Check your math calculations by doing the problem on another part of the paper.

55. Draw and label a picture or diagram if you feel it will be helpful to you.

56. Use accurately labeled pictures and diagrams to bring to mind a procedure for dealing with a problem.

57. Convert numerical information into forms that are meaningful for *you*.

58. To avoid thinking in abstractions, substitute simple numbers for symbols.

59. Check your math calculations by doing the problem another way, including backwards if possible.

60. When you are doing math calculations, be careful to put down the correct numbers. Copy accurately.

61. In doing math problems that call for calculation, remember that you are looking for *one* correct answer. Although other answers may be close, there is never more than one right answer to the particular problem.

62. On tests of your numerical ability, note carefully key words, terms, and data included in the questions.

63. Practice estimating answers when using practice materials. This keeps you in the ball park of the right answer.

64. If you know a second language, use it to help you make sense out of unfamiliar words in English.

65. Guess if you don't know the answer and you have more to gain than to lose.

66. It is possible to make quantitative comparisons even though actual numbers are not given because the partial information provided is enough to compare.

67. Guess when you can eliminate enough answer choices to put the odds in your favor.

68. If you have only a small bit of information about a specific question, you should make an "informed guess" after eliminating as many answer choices as possible.

69. On a matching test, always guess after you have matched all the items you know.

70. Because there is rarely a penalty for guessing on true-false tests, always guess if you do not know an answer.

71. If you are still undecided among two or more answer choices, always guess instead of leaving the question unanswered.

72. Always guess when there is no penalty.

73. Know the specific characteristics of multiple-choice tests.

74. Look for clues and giveaways, especially in nonstandardized tests.

75. In reading and vocabularly tests, if you don't know the word, make an educated guess.

76. Look for specific determiners such as *always, none, never.*

77. Be alert to contextual clues in sentence completion questions, using such words as *however, nevertheless, furthermore, on the contrary, in conclusion, finally,* and *consequently.*

78. Become familiar with commonly used prefixes and suffixes.

79. Look for overlapping questions in which one choice automatically includes another.

80. Look for verbal clues.

81. Look for patterns in nonverbal questions using number series or letter series.

Remember That . . .

82. True-false questions with absolute qualifiers such as *always* or *never* are more likely to be false than true.

83. The longer a true-false statement, the more likely that it will be true.

84. If any part of a statement is false, then the whole statement is false.

85. True-false questions must be either absolutely true or absolutely false without qualifications or exceptions.

86. When you are dealing with rankings and orderings there is usually a spread on either side of a correct answer involving dates or quantities.

87. A matching test is a recognition test that calls for associating or matching one fact or concept with another.

88. Most matching questions do not include trivia, so it is important to concentrate your study on important topics and facts.

89. There is usually a common theme between the question list and the answer list in a matching test, so it is often helpful to eliminate answers that do not fit the theme.

90. It is important to clearly understand the directions for matching the items on the two lists.

91. Matching tests usually deal with such things as dates and events, people and contributions, terms and definitions, authors and titles.

92. Short-answer tests usually measure recall, so they focus on important facts, events, dates, names, concepts, formulas, and so on.

93. In preparing for an essay examination, it is important to review the major ideas emphasized by the instructor.

94. Finding out what criteria will be used to grade your essay answers is helpful for deciding on your approach.

95. Writing an outline for an essay question—allowing one half of the total time for outlining, and one half for writing—helps you produce a coherent essay that shows what you know.

96. Budgeting your time when writing essay test answers helps you allot time in proportion to the value of each question.

97. Looking for key words in essay questions can help focus your answers. Some examples of key words are: *contrast, trace, illustrate, explain, discuss, criticize, define, evaluate.*

98. In answering essay questions, you should write a clearly stated introduction in which you present your thesis, theme, or topic sentence. The body of your essay must support your theme, and facts should be used to support your viewpoint.

99. Checking your answers to an essay question for content, organization, grammar, punctuation, spelling, and sentence structure can turn a good essay into an excellent one.

100. Believe in yourself.

TEST TALK

Words and Phrases Used
in Test Directions and Test Bulletins

Before you begin the more detailed list of testing terms, be sure that you understand the following six basic definitions:

test	A selection of tasks that you perform to demonstrate your knowledge of or skill in something
battery	A group of tests taken together
answer sheet	A separate piece of printed paper on which you mark your answers to multiple-choice test questions
item	One whole task in a test, containing both the question or problem and the answer choices, if any
stem	The question part of an item; the question or problem or incomplete statement that comes before the answer choices
response	The answer part of an item; the multiple choices, the filled-in blanks, the word or phrase you supply to answer the question in the stem

What follows is an alphabetical list of terms used in test bulletins, in the directions that examiners give when they administer tests, and in the internal directions printed in the tests themselves.

ability test	A test of one or more generalized learning skills such as reading, writing, and arithmetic
achievement test	A test of your knowledge, recall, and skill in a school subject like reading, math, or history
administration	The giving of a test to several people at one time is called a test administration.

admissions test	A test used to select applicants for admission to secondary school, college, or graduate school
analogy item	A kind of test question that asks you to find the relationship between one pair of terms or ideas and apply that relationship in selecting a similar pair
analyze	A test direction that means to explain all sides or parts of something and how they relate to each other and to themselves as a whole
answer space	The small space on an answer sheet that you blacken with your pencil to show the letter or number of an answer you've chosen; usually a very small box, or oval (sometimes called a "bubble"), or pair of parallel lines
antonym item	A kind of test question that asks you to select a word that is most nearly opposite in meaning to a given word
aptitude test	A type of test you take to demonstrate certain skills (academic, mechanical, clerical, and so on) that you've learned over a long period of time. This test is used to predict how well you will do in a particular situation such as college or a job.
basic skills	The main skills you learned in elementary school: reading, writing, and arithmetic ("the 3 R's")
bubble	One of the kinds of answer spaces on a printed answer sheet
bulletin of information	When used in connection with testing, this term always refers to a publication written for those who are going to take a certain test. It describes the test and explains where and when it will be given.
calendar	This term is used most often in connection with large testing programs like ACT and the College Board; the testing calendar usually comes with the bulletin of information and shows not only when the tests will be given but also when you register to take them.
candidate	Used in tests for admission to some institutions, this word means a person who is going to take a test. Some testing programs publish a "Bulletin for Candidates."
clerical test	A special kind of test to let you show your skill in certain kinds of office tasks such as filing, sorting, and looking up things. Sometimes a clerical test will include demonstrations of skill in typing and shorthand.
college placement	A process by which colleges assign students to courses that are appropriate for them. They often use placement tests for this purpose.
compare (or contrast)	Point out similarities or differences.

completion item	A test item in which you fill in some information that is missing, a word or phrase or a number that will make a stem a complete and accurate statement
demonstrate	Use examples or evidence to support your answer.
describe	Show in words what something is like and include examples.
discuss	Present all sides of a subject in detail.
essay test	A test in which you write out your answer to a question or a problem in complete sentences or paragraphs (no choice of answers given)
evaluate	Give your opinion and support it.
examinee	The person taking a test
examiner	The person giving the test
free-response item	Any test item in which you write out your response to a question or problem instead of choosing a response from among several given
grid	That part of an electronically scored answer sheet in which you translate letters or numbers into machine language by blackening spaces, ovals, or circles that correspond to each letter or number. (See Section 2 on the practice answer sheet in the back of the book.) Some examiners may use this word as a verb, too, and tell you to "grid your name" on the answer sheet.
I.D.	A document (such as your driver's license) that will identify you at a testing center
identify	List or name something.
intelligence test	The old-fashioned name for a test of assorted intellectual skills learned in school and at home
interest inventory	An organized collection of questions and problems and illustrations to help you understand and think about what your particular interests in life might be at the present time
interpretation	The process of deciding what a certain test score means and the results of that decision
I.Q.	The name given to a score earned on an intelligence test. The letters stand for intelligence quotient and express a ratio between the score you earn and the score that a person of your age might be expected to earn. (I.Q. is only a test score, like all other test scores, and is not a human characteristic.)
matching item	A test item in which your task is to match one given date or fact or name with something else

mathematical test	The name given to all tests of skill in numerical tasks, from grade school arithmetic to the most advanced mathematics
mental ability test	Another name for intelligence test (see above)
mental maturity test	Still another name for intelligence test
multiple-choice item	A test task in which you are to choose the best answer to a question from among a set of four or five options listed right after the stem
name grid	See "grid"
norms	Tables of information that in some way rank the test scores of many people. The "norm" is exactly the middle or average score earned by a large group. If your score is higher than the average of other people, you are said to be "above the norm." Obviously, only half of the people in any group can be above the norm.
numerical test	Same meaning as mathematical test except that it more often has to do with simpler mathematics such as arithmetic
open-book test	A test in which you can look up answers in your textbook and other references as you work
option	One of the answer choices in the list of four or five given in a multiple-choice item
outline	List the important points under headings and subheadings.
percentile rank	The proportion of people in 100 who earned a score lower than yours when they took the same test. If the percentile rank of your score is 63, it means that 63 percent of the people in the comparison group earned scores lower than yours.
placement	See college placement.
psychological test	In most of the circumstances in which you are likely to encounter a psychological test, the term means a test of your skills in verbal and mathematical and reasoning tasks (like a mental ability test) and not a test of your psychological characteristics.
proctor	An assistant to the examiner in administering a test to a large group of people
registration	In large, controlled testing programs like the College Board's, you apply ahead of time to take certain tests at a certain place and receive a ticket that gets you into the testing center to take those tests. This process is called "registration."

registration number	The identification number you receive in the registration process, sometimes printed on a set of labels
sample item	The item shown at the beginning of a test to illustrate how the items in the test are to be answered
scratch work	The writing or figuring you do, usually on a piece of paper separate from your test booklet or answer sheet, while you take a test
scholarship test	A test you take as a part of the competition for a scholarship grant
selection test	A test used by a college or an employer as an aid in selecting individuals for admission or employment (see "admission test")
skim	To look over a sentence or paragraph or other form of reading matter, reading only the key words, to find the general idea of it
speeded test	A test that few people are expected to finish in the time allowed; a test in which the speed of your work as well as its accuracy is counted
standardized test	A test that is given in exactly the same form to many people
stanine	A score reported on a scale that is divided into nine segments. Each such score is expressed as a number from one to nine.
student booklet	The test booklet used by the person taking the test
synonym item	A test item that asks you to choose a word that is closest in meaning to a given word
take-home test	A test that you are permitted to carry out of the testing room, answer as best you can according to rules laid down by the examiner, and bring back later
task	The question or problem in a test that you are supposed to answer or solve (see "item")
test center	The place where you take a test or a series of tests, usually in a large testing program
ticket of admission	The ticket you use to gain admittance to a test center to take a test for which you have registered ahead of time
trace	Organize events according to when they happened.
true-false test	A test, usually a long one containing many items, in which there are just two optional answers for each question: true and false

THE PRACTICE TEST

If you haven't taken an objective test for a long time and are therefore a little rusty, or if an electronically scored separate answer sheet is unfamiliar to you, the practice test that begins on page 107 may be a worthwhile thing for you to spend some time on. The test is based on information in this book. The practice test is designed to:

1. Give you practice in reviewing for a test;

2. Give you practice in answering multiple-choice questions;

3. Give you practice in filling out an answer sheet;

4. Give you some clues about what you have learned in this book;

5. Give you an idea of the parts of this book you need to study some more.

What is the practice test like? Here is some of the information about the practice test you'll want to know before you take it:

1. What does it cover? Since this is a how-to-do-it book about taking a test, the practice test concentrates on the how-to-do-it chapters of the book (2, 3, 4, 5, and 7).

2. What kind of test will it be? It will consist of 40 multiple-choice questions with four answer choices given for each question.

3. How long will it be? The test is not a timed test, so take as much time as you need to complete it, but set aside at least an hour of time without interruptions for your own testing period.

4. How will you answer the questions? By choosing one of the four answer choices as the BEST answer for each question, then black-

ening the space that indicates the letter of that answer on your answer sheet.

5. How will the test be scored? You will score the answer sheet with the key provided after you have completed the test. You will not add up your "score" as a number, but will use your wrong answers as guides to which parts of this book you should read again.

6. Will there be penalties for guessing? No. Answer every question.

7. Will spelling and handwriting count? No. Not if your name can be read.

8. What supplies will you need when you take the test? Only a No. 2 pencil and an eraser. (Ballpoint pens cause problems if you change your mind about an answer.)

What to do first. Here is the way to proceed:

1. Carefully remove the answer sheet (pages 115-116). Turn it so that the spaces for name and address are at the top as you look at it.

2. Look at the section headed "Sample Fill-in" on page 116. Your first job in taking the test is to use the spaces on page 115 to describe yourself in the same ways as John Smith has described himself in the sample—using letters and numbers that fit you.

   a. In Box 1 PRINT your name, last name first, on the first line;

   b. Then print your complete address on the second and third lines;

   c. If you were taking this test at a test center, you'd complete the fourth line by giving the city the center is in and the number of the center, which would be provided by the person administering the test.

   d. Print today's date—month, day, and year—on the last line;

   e. In Box 2 print the first four letters of your last name in the spaces indicated, then your first initial and your middle initial;

   f. Now "code" your name and initials by blackening the appropriate oval under each letter you have printed.

   g. In Box 3, code the month, day, and year of your birth in the same way as you coded your name, using the last two digits of the year.

   h. In Box 4, code your sex by blackening the appropriate oval.

i. In Box 5, first print and then code the "registration number" that will identify your answer sheet. (For the purpose of this practice test, pretend that your registration number is 4-5-3-6 -0-2-7.)

j. Have someone else check out your identification coding in boxes 2, 3, 4 and 5, either now or later, so you can make sure that you've handled this operation properly.

3. Now get ready to mark your answers to the practice test down the right-hand side of the answer sheet, in the section headed "Practice Test."

4. Finally, turn to page 107 of this book and begin taking the test. Don't hurry. You can come back to difficult questions as often as you wish.

After you finish the test. (1) First, score your responses. Lay your marked answer sheet beside the answer key (page 117). Compare the answers marked on your answer sheet with the correct answers given in the key and draw a circle on your answer sheet around the number of every question you have answered wrong. (2) Next to every answer on your answer sheet is a page reference that tells you where in the book you can find the correct answer. Go back into the book right away, locate the correct answer for every question you missed in the test, and mark that correct answer with a big X on your answer sheet. Just this much attention to the answers you missed will help you a great deal to remember the correct answer next time. (3) Keep this book and answer sheet for a quick review of how to take a test before each new test you take.

PRACTICE TEST

Directions: This test consists of 40 multiple-choice questions about things discussed in this book. Each question has four possible answers. For each question, choose what you think is the BEST answer of the four given and mark the space on the answer sheet to show the letter of your choice. You may start when you are ready.

1. Which of the following probably is NOT something important to ask about a test ahead of time?

   (A) What will the test cover?
   (B) Who will be administering the test?
   (C) What kind of test will it be?
   (D) Will there be a penalty for guessing?

2. You are about to take a test that is to be given in schools all over the state. Who will be good sources of information about the test beforehand?

   (A) Teachers
   (B) Counselors
   (C) Principal
   (D) All of the above

3. You have been a licensed beautician in another state and know that you have to take a test to obtain a license in your new state of residence. What or who will be the best source of information about that test?

   (A) The beauty shop you patronize
   (B) Other beauticians you know
   (C) The nearest beauty school
   (D) The licensing agency

107

4. What is the *ideal* way to prepare for a test?

(A) Review in an organized way with a group of friends.
(B) Keep up with assignments and review all year.
(C) Cram with a plan.
(D) Review in a group session just before the test.

5. After you find out all you can about what the coming test will be like, what should you do *next* in preparation?

(A) Ask your friends what they think will be in the test.
(B) Underline topic sentences in the textbook.
(C) Go through your notes.
(D) Decide what to review.

6. What kinds of things should be at the top of your "priority list" of topics for review?

(A) Things that are likely to be in the test that you know pretty well
(B) Things that everyone agrees are sure to be in the test
(C) Things that are likely to be in the test that you don't know
(D) Things that you cannot predict will be in the test

7. Which of the following is/are likely to be a good source or good sources of clues as to what will be in an upcoming test?

(A) The teacher
(B) Your notes on what the teacher has emphasized
(C) Other students' expectations based on their notes
(D) Choices (B) and (C) above

8. Which of the following is NOT mentioned in the book as a good source of review material?

(A) Reports you have written
(B) Your own lecture notes
(C) Other students' lecture notes
(D) Textbooks and references

9. If you are going to take an academic aptitude or ability test like the SAT or ACT, which of the following methods is the best for finding out what the test will be like?

(A) Read the bulletins about the tests published by their sponsors.
(B) Find people who have taken the test and ask them.
(C) Ask as many teachers as you can.
(D) Ask your counselor to tell you what the test is like.

10. The book recommends a rap session with fellow students to bring into focus your expectation of what a test will be like. How much time do you need to devote to such a rap session?

    (A) Not more than a few minutes
    (B) Several sessions of two hours each
    (C) All day, counting interruptions
    (D) A couple of hours, if you take it seriously

11. The author of this book stresses the importance of building a review plan or priority list when you start your preparation for a test. Which of the following is NOT one of the reasons given for recommending this?

    (A) Just getting ready accomplishes part of your review.
    (B) Reviewing this way increases your chances of not being surprised.
    (C) Reviewing this way covers the important things in the least time.
    (D) Reviewing this way is the best way to prepare for a test.

12. You discover that a large part of an upcoming test is likely to require recall of specific facts. How should you review in order to remember facts like names and dates?

    (A) Memorize facts as you go along in your total review.
    (B) Set them aside for review and memorization in a cram session.
    (C) Reread the notes or books in which the facts appear.
    (D) Read the topic sentences in the paragraphs containing the facts.

13. Where is the topic sentence found most often in a paragraph?

    (A) First sentence in the paragraph
    (B) Last sentence in the paragraph
    (C) Almost anywhere in the paragraph
    (D) All of the above

14. What else besides the topic sentences should be underlined in your text (if you own it) during a review?

    (A) Nothing
    (B) Everything but adjectives and adverbs
    (C) Section headings
    (D) Names and dates

15. Why is a *second* rap session a good idea?

    (A) To answer the questions you raised during your review
    (B) To pick the brains of the better-prepared students
    (C) To share your information with others
    (D) To build rapport among the group to be tested

16. What is the author's opinion of cramming before a test?

    (A) It helps by condensing review into a short time.
    (B) Done correctly, it's the best way to learn certain limited things.
    (C) It often makes up for neglected study.
    (D) It should be done a day or two before the test.

17. With regard to cramming, the author of this book is

    (A) very specific, listing eight suggested steps
    (B) approving, but not too specific on how to cram
    (C) reluctant to approve, but lists some general techniques
    (D) disapproving, suggesting that cramming is a waste of time

18. What is one of the first things to do in preparation for an upcoming essay test made by your teacher?

    (A) Review your grammar, particularly subjects and predicates.
    (B) Practice your handwriting.
    (C) Find out what the teacher's favorite essay topics are.
    (D) Review the spelling of words that are difficult for you.

19. Who is likely to be the best source of information about possible topics in an essay test to be given by the state or an outside agency?

    (A) Your teacher in the subject to be tested
    (B) Your academic counselor
    (C) The bulletins of the agency
    (D) Other students in your class

20. Which of the following is the best thing to do if someone offers to sell you a copy of an upcoming important test, or the answers to it?

    (A) Buy the test and report the seller to the authorities.
    (B) Ask to examine the test before you buy it.
    (C) Find out how that person obtained the test.
    (D) Save your money. (It's bound to be a fake.)

21. Which of the following is good advice to take before you take a test?

    (A) Get a good night's sleep.
    (B) Stay away from coffee and drugs.
    (C) Don't eat or drink much.
    (D) All of the above

22. What is probably the most important thing to do while taking a test?

    (A) Choose a seat with good light and ventilation.
    (B) Refrain from talking.
    (C) Give the test your complete attention.
    (D) Listen carefully to all instructions.

23. What is the best time to ask questions after you are in the testing room?

    (A) When the examiner first comes into the testing room
    (B) When the examiner asks, "Are there any questions?"
    (C) While the examiner is passing out the tests
    (D) After the test has started and the group has settled down

24. What is the best way to ask a question about the test procedure after the test has begun?

    (A) Don't risk asking at all.
    (B) Ask in a soft voice after raising your hand.
    (C) Raise your hand and wait for the examiner to come to you.
    (D) Ask your neighbor in a whisper.

25. If you feel that you have good cause for complaint about the way a testing session is being run, what is important to remember about complaining?

    (A) You can always complain later.
    (B) Wait a day or two, then talk it over calmly with your teacher.
    (C) Object mildly at the time, but don't press the issue.
    (D) All of the above

26. Why does the author of the book advise you not to attempt to cheat on a test?

    (A) Cheating is difficult to get away with.
    (B) It is not worth the risk and it's a serious violation.
    (C) It is contrary to the rules of a democracy.
    (D) Test-givers know all the methods of cheating.

27. What does the author think is the hardest-to-understand part of an electronically scored answer sheet?

    (A) Keeping your place so your answers match the questions
    (B) Keeping your marks black and heavy and between the lines
    (C) The coding of name and identification
    (D) Avoiding stray marks on the answer sheet

28. Which of the following is LEAST important to find out before a test?

    (A) What is the penalty for guessing, if any?
    (B) How much time will I have to work on the test?
    (C) Do I have to answer the questions in the order given?
    (D) What will the test cover?

29. What is the MOST important technique that the author recommends for taking any multiple-choice test?

    (A) Answer the questions as they come in the test booklet.
    (B) Answer first all the questions that are easy for you.
    (C) Give an equal amount of time to every question.
    (D) On the first pass, guess at the answers you are not sure of.

30. What should you try to accomplish on a *second* pass through a test?

    (A) Try to eliminate some of the answer choices you know are wrong.
    (B) Answer every question, even if you have to guess.
    (C) Make your answer sheet neat and free of stray marks.
    (D) Check your coding of identifying information.

31. On a test in which there is no penalty for guessing, what should you do about questions on which you don't even have any hunches?

    (A) Mark an answer for every question in the test.
    (B) Guess only when you can eliminate one choice.
    (C) Don't guess.
    (D) Guess only when you can eliminate two choices.

32. On a test in which three points are *subtracted* from your score for every wrong answer, when should you guess?

   (A) Not at all
   (B) When you can eliminate one of the answer choices
   (C) When you can eliminate half of the answer choices
   (D) When you know the correct answers by hunch

33. According to the author, which of the following actions is an efficient use of time in a test-taking situation?

   (A) Reading the answer choices only until you find the correct choice.
   (B) Saving a few minutes for checking over your answer sheet.
   (C) Spending the same amount of time on each test question.
   (D) Doing the hardest questions first.

34. What is the FIRST thing you should do in an essay test?

   (A) Read all of the questions or topics carefully.
   (B) Jot down on a piece of paper the ideas that occur to you.
   (C) Indicate on the paper which topics you are writing about.
   (D) Figure out how much time you can devote to each topic.

35. What is the SECOND thing you should do in an essay test?

   (A) Make notes to yourself on things to say on each topic.
   (B) Choose topics on which you can write clearly and knowledgeably.
   (C) Divide the number of minutes by the number of topics.
   (D) Allow some time at the end of the test to read over your work.

36. In the 1-2-3 sequence of steps in starting an essay test, what is the THIRD thing you do?

   (A) Make quick notes to yourself about things to say on each topic.
   (B) Start the first paragraph of your first topic.
   (C) Indicate which topic you are writing about.
   (D) Allocate your time for each topic.

37. The first sentence in a paragraph is the topic sentence and it should

    (A) Lay out the logic of the paragraph
    (B) Summarize what is in the paragraph
    (C) State the major point of the paragraph
    (D) Contain the strongest evidence

38. Which of the following is NOT what you should do in writing an essay test?

    (A) Write a long paragraph that contains specific examples supporting several ideas.
    (B) Write in complete and short sentences, making sure that each has a subject and predicate.
    (C) Create your own answers to one or more questions on different subjects.
    (D) Pay attention to grammar, spelling, and correct usage.

39. If you think that you know nothing about an essay topic, you should stay calm and do which of the following?

    (A) Write about some other topic as if you misunderstood the directions.
    (B) Put what pieces of information you have into outline form.
    (C) Say you don't know anything and go on to the next topic.
    (D) Write several long paragraphs as if you really did know a lot about the topic.

40. When you really want to learn something from a test you take, which of the following is the FIRST thing to do after the test is over?

    (A) Review the test right away with others who took it.
    (B) Review the test by yourself.
    (C) Review with your teachers.
    (D) Try to get to see the test and your answer sheet.

END OF THE PRACTICE TEST. CHECK OVER YOUR WORK.

When you've completed the practice test (when you've answered every question and checked over your answer sheet for possible errors), use the answer key on page 117 to score your answers.

This is the answer sheet for the Practice Test that begins on page 107. When you are ready to take the Practice Test, carefully remove this answer sheet from the book. You'll find instructions for filling it in on pages 104 and 105.

FILL IN TO DESCRIBE YOURSELF

USE ONLY A SOFT LEAD PENCIL (NO. 2) FOR COMPLETING THIS ANSWER SHEET. DO NOT USE INK OR BALL-POINT PEN.

PRACTICE TEST

1.

YOUR NAME: _____
(PRINT)   LAST   FIRST   MIDDLE

HOME ADDRESS: _____
(PRINT)   NUMBER AND STREET

_____
CITY   STATE   ZIP CODE

CENTER: _____
(PRINT)   CITY   NUMBER

DATE OF TESTING: ___/___/___
MONTH DAY YEAR

2. YOUR NAME

FIRST 4 LETTERS OF LAST NAME | F.I. | M.I.

3. DATE OF BIRTH

MONTH | DAY | YEAR

JAN. FEB. MAR. APR. MAY JUNE JULY AUG. SEPT. OCT. NOV. DEC.

4. SEX

MALE ○

FEMALE ○

5. REGISTRATION NUMBER

1 Ⓐ Ⓑ Ⓒ Ⓓ
2 Ⓐ Ⓑ Ⓒ Ⓓ
3 Ⓐ Ⓑ Ⓒ Ⓓ
4 Ⓐ Ⓑ Ⓒ Ⓓ
5 Ⓐ Ⓑ Ⓒ Ⓓ
6 Ⓐ Ⓑ Ⓒ Ⓓ
7 Ⓐ Ⓑ Ⓒ Ⓓ
8 Ⓐ Ⓑ Ⓒ Ⓓ
9 Ⓐ Ⓑ Ⓒ Ⓓ
10 Ⓐ Ⓑ Ⓒ Ⓓ
11 Ⓐ Ⓑ Ⓒ Ⓓ
12 Ⓐ Ⓑ Ⓒ Ⓓ
13 Ⓐ Ⓑ Ⓒ Ⓓ
14 Ⓐ Ⓑ Ⓒ Ⓓ
15 Ⓐ Ⓑ Ⓒ Ⓓ
16 Ⓐ Ⓑ Ⓒ Ⓓ
17 Ⓐ Ⓑ Ⓒ Ⓓ
18 Ⓐ Ⓑ Ⓒ Ⓓ
19 Ⓐ Ⓑ Ⓒ Ⓓ
20 Ⓐ Ⓑ Ⓒ Ⓓ
21 Ⓐ Ⓑ Ⓒ Ⓓ
22 Ⓐ Ⓑ Ⓒ Ⓓ
23 Ⓐ Ⓑ Ⓒ Ⓓ
24 Ⓐ Ⓑ Ⓒ Ⓓ
25 Ⓐ Ⓑ Ⓒ Ⓓ
26 Ⓐ Ⓑ Ⓒ Ⓓ
27 Ⓐ Ⓑ Ⓒ Ⓓ
28 Ⓐ Ⓑ Ⓒ Ⓓ
29 Ⓐ Ⓑ Ⓒ Ⓓ
30 Ⓐ Ⓑ Ⓒ Ⓓ
31 Ⓐ Ⓑ Ⓒ Ⓓ
32 Ⓐ Ⓑ Ⓒ Ⓓ
33 Ⓐ Ⓑ Ⓒ Ⓓ
34 Ⓐ Ⓑ Ⓒ Ⓓ
35 Ⓐ Ⓑ Ⓒ Ⓓ
36 Ⓐ Ⓑ Ⓒ Ⓓ
37 Ⓐ Ⓑ Ⓒ Ⓓ
38 Ⓐ Ⓑ Ⓒ Ⓓ
39 Ⓐ Ⓑ Ⓒ Ⓓ
40 Ⓐ Ⓑ Ⓒ Ⓓ

SAMPLE FILL - IN

USE ONLY A SOFT LEAD PENCIL (NO. 2) FOR COMPLETING THIS ANSWER SHEET.
DO NOT USE INK OR BALL-POINT PEN.

1.

YOUR NAME: *SMITH   JOHN   E*
(PRINT)   LAST   FIRST   MIDDLE

HOME ADDRESS: *1947   CENTER   ST.*
(PRINT)   NUMBER AND STREET

EVANSTON   NJ   08540
                CITY   STATE   ZIP CODE

CENTER: *TRENTON   745*
(PRINT)   CITY   NUMBER

DATE OF TESTING: *6 | 10 | 80*
                MONTH   DAY   YEAR

---

2. YOUR NAME

FIRST 4 LETTERS OF LAST NAME				F. I.	M. I.
S	M	I	T	J	E

3. DATE OF BIRTH

MONTH	DAY		YEAR	
JAN.	1	8	6	3

4. SEX

MALE ●
FEMALE ○

5. REGISTRATION NUMBER

3 4 2 5 1 4 6

Please do NOT read this page until after you've taken the practice test. When you've done the best you can on the practice test, marking an answer for every question and checking over your answer sheet, turn the book around so that the other end of this page is at the top as you look at it and follow directions.

ANSWER KEY FOR THE PRACTICE TEST

The columns below indicate the correct answers for all questions in the practice test plus a page number for each question that shows where in the book that correct answer is discussed.

Lay your marked answer sheet beside this page and compare your answers with the answers given in this key. Draw a circle around the number of every question for which your answer is wrong and write in the space next to it the number of the page in the book where the correct answer is discussed. This whole process is part of learning how to take a test.

Question Number	Correct Answer	Page Reference	Question Number	Correct Answer	Page Reference
1	B	12	21	D	28
2	D	16	22	C	28
3	D	17	23	B	32
4	B	21	24	C	32
5	D	21	25	D	32
6	C	22	26	B	34
7	D	23	27	C	38
8	C	22	28	C	12
9	A	21	29	B	41
10	D	22	30	A	41
11	D	23	31	A	42
12	B	24	32	A	42
13	A	23	33	B	40
14	C	23	34	A	44
15	A	24	35	B	45
16	B	24	36	A	45
17	A	24	37	C	45
18	C	27	38	A	46
19	A	27	39	B	46
20	D	27	40	A	85

INDEX